P9-APP-215

PRAISE FOR *MARKETING IN THE #FAKENEWS ERA* AND PETER HORST

Marketing in the #FakeNews Era is a must-read book for any marketer today. The brands my agency works on have been built over decades and it only takes one misstep today to erase all of that equity. Peter Horst tackles some of the hardest questions we face today as brand builders. We must decide not just what a brand stands for but what a brand is willing to fight for.

PAUL GUNNING

CEO of DDB Chicago

Now more than ever, due to the charged political landscape, marketers must be deliberate about the actions and messages they undertake on behalf of their brands. In *Marketing in the #FakeNews Era*, esteemed CMO Peter Horst gives timely and practical advice to marketers as they influence not only their marketing organizations, but their entire enterprise. *Marketing in the #FakeNews Era* will help any company thrive in this environment where the lines between the business and political landscape have blurred.

DEBORA BEACHNER TOMLIN

EVP of Customer Experience and Marketing, CSAA Insurance Group

Peter Horst is an insightful marketer that is passionate about modernizing marketing for the digital age and driving long-term brand growth. He knows how to simplify what is complex and *Marketing in the #FakeNews Era* brings this expertise by providing a practical and eye-opening roadmap around navigating the complexity of nurturing one's brand reputation. For any professional that shares the responsibility of building, protecting, or growing brands, *Marketing in the #FakeNews Era* is required reading.

RONALEE ZARATE-BAYANI

Chief Marketing Officer of Los Angeles Rams

Peter is an inspirational leader and truly authentic marketer. He has that rare combination of an impressive strategic vision along with an ability to challenge teams to deliver results in support of that vision. Peter's ability to tell a compelling story to develop strategy is unparalleled. I worked with Peter for over ten years at Capital One where his leadership drove groundbreaking innovation in marketing, product development, customer experience, and brand development. He deeply cares about people, as well as the business, and is always working to develop the team while delivering business results.

STEVE JAMES

Senior Vice President of Strategy, Insights, and Marketing, Fannie Mae

Peter is a "big idea" executive. He was transformative in moving what was mostly a service-oriented business to a recurring subscription-based revenue model (long before the concept of SaaS was born) at TruSecure. He has an innate talent for taking big problems, breaking them down into manageable pieces and executing to positive results. I have used Peter over the years in my other business ventures and highly value his insight and guidance.

JOE SANDER
CEO of Arxan Technologies

Peter isn't just a speaker, he's a captivator. His depth of experience, engaging style, and story-telling abilities give him a one-of-a-kind capability to connect.

JOHN NEWALL
President of McKinney

Peter led an executive education session for some of Google's highest potential business leaders. In that session, Peter was supportive and inspirational as he translated his years of experience in building brands into clear and action-ready advice.

JAKE BREEDEN
Co-Founder of Sapien Experience

MARKETING IN THE #FAKENEWS ERA

MARKETING IN THE #FAKENEWS ERA

NEW RULES FOR A NEW REALITY OF TRIBALISM, ACTIVISM, AND LOSS OF TRUST

PETER HORST

Advantage®

Copyright © 2018 by Peter Horst.

All rights reserved. No part of this book may be used or reproduced in any manner whatsoever without prior written consent of the author, except as provided by the United States of America copyright law.

Published by Advantage, Charleston, South Carolina.
Member of Advantage Media Group.

ADVANTAGE is a registered trademark, and the Advantage colophon is a trademark of Advantage Media Group, Inc.

Printed in the United States of America.

10 9 8 7 6 5 4 3 2 1

ISBN: 978-1-59932-926-0
LCCN: 2018942263

Cover design by Carly Blake.
Layout design by Megan Elger.

This publication is designed to provide accurate and authoritative information in regard to the subject matter covered. It is sold with the understanding that the publisher is not engaged in rendering legal, accounting, or other professional services. If legal advice or other expert assistance is required, the services of a competent professional person should be sought.

Advantage Media Group is proud to be a part of the Tree Neutral® program. Tree Neutral offsets the number of trees consumed in the production and printing of this book by taking proactive steps such as planting trees in direct proportion to the number of trees used to print books. To learn more about Tree Neutral, please visit **www.treeneutral.com**.

Advantage Media Group is a publisher of business, self-improvement, and professional development books and online learning. We help entrepreneurs, business leaders, and professionals share their Stories, Passion, and Knowledge to help others Learn & Grow. Do you have a manuscript or book idea that you would like us to consider for publishing? Please visit **advantagefamily.com** or call **1.866.775.1696**.

For Kris, Maddy, Kaela, Sam, and Gar.
And yes, the dogs, too.

TABLE OF CONTENTS

PART III: LEADING UNDER FIRE

ACKNOWLEDGMENTS

I want to start by thanking all the people who lent their thoughts and insights, which were so critical in putting this book together. Together, they represent an astounding brain trust of marketing leaders, reputation experts, academics, and all-around big thinkers.

Thanks first to all those who generously shared their experiences but preferred not to share their names, out of the understandable concern about speaking on the record about these sensitive issues. Even that took courage in this environment, and I appreciate their confidence. Others who spent time with me to offer their wisdom include Jeetendr Sehdev, Anthony Johndrow, Kevin Keller, Helaine Klasky, Sarah Rabia, Michael Maslansky, David Mayer, Maryam Banikarim, Lilliana Mason, Tony Pace, Christian Madsbjerg, Paul Argenti, Jennifer Saenz, David Mayer, Mark Ritson, Denise Karkos, Jeff Rosenblum, Ralph Santana, Nick Primola, Mike Paul, Jim Link, and Kim Whitler. Deepest thanks to all of you.

Thanks also to my editorial team at Advantage|ForbesBooks. Although I've launched dozens, if not hundreds, of new products in my career, this book was a first for me, and their help was invaluable.

Finally, and most importantly, thanks to my wife, Kris. She was insistent that I actually take the time to write this book and she provided enthusiastic motivation, unwavering moral support, and valuable editorial input through the project. In so many ways, I couldn't have done it without her.

WELCOME TO THE NEW REALITY

"I can't wait to hear what you learn—just don't mention me."

I was preparing for an upcoming speech on the topic of how brands are increasingly drawn into social and political firestorms, #boycotts, and social media crises. To do that, I spoke with a number of executives who had lived through such episodes of controversy and turmoil. One was a high-profile CMO, an old friend who had worked for me in a past life and had lived through more than his share of very public brand brushfires. He shared his experiences, and I in turn related some of the learning I was starting to gather from other beleaguered marketers.

"I'm so glad you're doing this—it's a really important subject," he said. "Make sure to let me know what you learn from the other CMOs." He paused and then added sheepishly, "Just whatever you do, don't mention me."

Wait, what?

CMOs are generally not a shy and retiring group and don't usually request anonymity. When I had the same conversation with several other seasoned marketers, that's when I realized I had to write this book. When veteran executives say they really want to read something but are afraid to be associated with it, you know it's a topic that needs some attention.

> When veteran executives say they really want to read something but are afraid to be associated with it, you know it's a topic that needs some attention.

I've been a marketer for three decades, for everything from popcorn to brokerage, chocolate bars to checking accounts, and cable TV to cybersecurity, working at the likes of General Mills, Hershey, Capital One, TD Ameritrade, and others. The one consistent theme that ran throughout that magical mystery tour of a career path was this: building powerful, breakthrough brands that tapped into popular culture. Sometimes it was about building a brand from the ground up, as in the case of the birth of Ameritrade (pre-TD) and creating cultishly popular ad campaigns. Other times it was about taking an already strong brand to the next level, as in moving Capital One from credit card issuer to diversified financial giant. There were also the familiar household names that just needed new life and energy breathed into them, as in giving Jolly Rancher a total reboot for a new generation.

And if there's one skill that helped me along the way, it was a knack for connecting the dots between disparate forces bubbling up in the market and turning that insight into rocket fuel for my brand. Success or failure often comes down to simply being one step ahead of a trend and two parts more creative than a competitor.

During my career, I've dealt with more than my share of challenging environments. My first role in marketing was working on Nature Valley Granola Bars. At that time there was a broad-based campaign against coconut oil, and we raced to reformulate the line (only to see coconut oil become a health food product years later). At Ameritrade we got called out by consumer advocates who felt we were encouraging unsound trading by financial amateurs. Years later, I was at Capital One during the banking crisis, when banks became everyone's favorite whipping boy for any number of sins. So I certainly knew what it was like to manage a brand under fire.

But I've never seen anything like the current reality. These days, brand and reputation stewards face an unprecedented set of risks; their brand can be swept up at a moment's notice into a social or political crisis they never saw coming. A perfect storm of forces has created an environment where brands can instantly become this week's focus for indignant and increasingly activist consumers, energized social media influencers, and news media hungry for headlines.

This is the #FakeNews Era. While it's tempting in many respects to call it the "Trump Era," as many analysts and pundits do, the truth is this new reality predates the 45th president and will certainly persist beyond his term—however long that may be.

I've also never seen anything like the anxiety that is causing so many senior executives to show eager interest in a topic they dare not discuss publicly. "Tell me what you learn, just don't use my name," was a refrain I heard over and over again. So that was all the motivation I needed to get serious about studying this new terrain and providing some guidelines for how leaders can survive and even thrive within it.

In Part I, New Reality, I examine the dynamics that marketers must understand and address in the #FakeNews Era. These include a deepening polarization across many aspects of society and a disappearance of the big, comfortable middle market that so many brands depend on. I also look at the dramatic rise of tribalism, loss of trust, and increase in fear that are driving so many of these new challenges. Making matters even more complicated, along with these new realities comes a growing expectation among increasingly activist consumers that brands and their companies step into the social/political fray to help make the world better.

In Part II, New Rules, I provide a framework and guidance for how to thoughtfully and sure-footedly navigate these turbulent and unfamiliar waters. The process begins with defining your core values and beliefs and deciding where and how you are—or aren't—willing to engage in issues beyond your base business. Having done that, I explain how to thoroughly understand the tribes that ultimately determine your brand's fate, as well as ensure that you've done the best job you can to incorporate the appropriate perspectives and sensibilities into your strategies. Finally, I walk through some of the more tactical considerations around how to execute marketing programs that put your values on display without putting your brand in harm's way.

In Part III, Leading Under Fire, I describe how to prepare for the kind of brand brushfire that has become all too common yet also unpredictable for brands in the #FakeNews Era. In the world of a nonstop news cycle and an energized, social-media–enabled public, you have to get your ducks in a row before the storm hits you. In the event your brand does get caught in a social/political swirl, I provide critical guidance on what to do and, just as importantly, what *not* to do when you're under fire. I close by looking at where this reality is going and whether we should hold out any hope of a warmer, sunnier day to come.

Although the word "marketing" is in the title, this book is not intended to be simply a how-to book for marketing practitioners. I wrote this book for the broad group of people who are accountable for the ongoing health and vitality of that critical corporate asset: the brand. That group certainly includes the marketers who define the strategies and build the campaigns that will either reinforce or undermine the company's brand equities and purposes.

But this book is also for the communications and PR professionals who focus more of their attention on corporate reputation, and who typically serve on the frontlines of battle when crisis hits. The classic PR playbook will not suffice in the #FakeNews Era, so communications professionals will need to thoroughly understand the new moves required for it. And more

> This book is also for the communications and PR professionals who focus more of their attention on corporate reputation, and who typically serve on the frontlines of battle when crisis hits.

than ever, both marketers and PR managers need a deep understanding of each other's craft, because another new reality is that brand health and corporate reputation have become deeply interwoven. Both functions need to operate with a rich appreciation for their respective needs and challenges. So I encourage both marketers and communications professionals to pay careful attention, not only to those sections most relevant to their craft, but also to their partner's.

Finally, with brand value driving so much of total enterprise value, this book should be read by anyone who is accountable for the long-term financial health of an organization. That means you, CEOs, general managers, and board members. There is a growing focus on the question of how we account for, steward, and publicly report on the value of brands, and the senior-most leaders will be increasingly asked what they've done to understand and protect that precious and fragile asset. From that perspective, you are all brand managers and should pay careful attention to the new realities for brands in the #FakeNews Era.

PART I:
NEW REALITY

CHAPTER 1

COLLAPSE OF THE MIDDLE AND THE RISE OF TRIBALISM

There's no question that the world changed in many ways on November 6, 2016. The election of Donald J. Trump was nothing if not surprising—stunning, really. The pollsters on the whole never saw it coming. News commentators were visibly shocked. Most of the nation was surprised—some thrilled and others dismayed. Everything about the candidate and his campaign was so unlike everything that had come before that most of us were utterly gobsmacked.

Regardless of which side of the political spectrum you sat on, this shock and awe was also accompanied by a feeling that somehow we were experiencing a huge change. We felt that norms were being upended, rules were being rewritten, and basic forces of nature were shifting before our eyes.

And while some of that sense of change can indeed be traced directly back to the 45th president, the truth is that the rise and election of Donald Trump is a symptom and an outcome of a set of forces that were already in play well before the 2016 election. These same forces shaped the environment that brands operate in and created the new risks they face, often generating some form of public controversy or social media crisis. Certainly, some of these episodes were prompted by the president himself, as well as his Twitter handle, but for the most part the treacherous brand landscape was defined by the same forces that carried Trump into office.

> The truth is that the rise and election of Donald Trump is a symptom and an outcome of a set of forces that were already in play well before the 2016 election.

These forces present organizations of most every type with a new reality—one that will very likely persist beyond Trump's term in office. Brand and reputation owners must fully understand this new reality and its implications in order to thoughtfully and successfully pursue their mission while steering clear of the risks.

The stakes have never been higher. On average, brand value alone contributes 19 percent of enterprise value, according to analysis by the Marketing Accountability Standards Board (MASB—the organization that focuses on establishing standards, metrics, and processes for evaluating marketing effectiveness). "For consumer-driven businesses, that number can easily exceed 50 percent of shareholder value," said Tony Pace, CEO of MASB and former CMO of Subway. "The question of who owns and who influences brand value within the corporate structure deserves renewed attention. For years, the CMO or senior marketer would say 'that's all mine.' Functionally, that may be true but has tended to leave growth of the brand, and its significant influence on enterprise value, outside the board of directors' responsibilities. Given the growth imperative, it is time to revisit that approach."

With so vast a proportion of the company's stock price riding on the health of the brand, preventing the brand from being dragged into social or political controversy is everybody's job—not just the marketing department's. So listen up, CEOs, boards, and shareholders. To help organizations more effectively shoulder that new burden, the Forbes Marketing Accountability Project is working in tandem with MASB to provide best practices benchmarks and guidance.

Let's look at the macro trends that helped set the stage for this new reality. We'll start by discussing broad societal forces like polarization, tribalism, and loss of trust, which all serve to heighten the energy levels and emotional tenor of the environment. When combined with consumers' increasing expectation for brands to step up and play a role in fixing society's problems, we get a high-risk environment where brands can be damned if they do jump in and lambasted if they don't.

In the following sections, we'll get more tactical and look at some of the new rules for managing brand and reputation in the new reality. I'll offer a framework for how to define your posture on the bigger issues. I'll also look at some cautionary tales and some success stories to illustrate the new moves you'll need to adopt in order to deftly manage these dynamics. Finally, with input from a group of marketing and reputation experts, I'll look at where this reality is going and whether we can hope for a return to the old normal.

COLLAPSE OF THE MIDDLE

I was sitting in my office in what used to be the original Hershey chocolate factory, in the middle of pastoral Hershey, Pennsylvania. I had just recently taken the role as Global CMO of the confectionery giant. It was an exciting chance to work with a stable of amazingly iconic brands, many with meaningful places in our culture and history. After all, Hershey is the "great American chocolate bar." Who doesn't have a warm, rosy memory of a melty, smushy s'more in summer, or know the simple joy of unwrapping a silver Kiss during the holidays? Hershey is just about as American as it gets, right alongside apple pie, baseball, and John Deere.

The problem was that the iconic bar, and several other venerable brands along with it, had just not been growing at the rate anyone wanted. After years of steady growth that delighted Wall Street, those broadly appealing brands were no longer clipping along at quite the same pace. And that lost volume was not going to giant competing brands. It was drifting away to the edges of the category: The artisanal, craft brands with the colorful founder stories. The daring culinary confections with bacon, cayenne pepper, and exotic crunchy bits. The organic, non-GMO, nothing artificial, sing-to-the-cacao-beans brands. The premium, pricey, wrap-it-in-gold-leaf chocolates. The big, broad middle was no longer the cool place to be.

> The big, broad middle was no longer the cool place to be.

Turns out that what I was seeing in the chocolate category was one of the most potent realities of the #FakeNews Era: the collapse of the middle. Pretty much everywhere you look, you can see evidence of a gradual polarization around a disappearing middle—whether that's the economic middle class, a centrist political posture, or a balanced and impartial news media. We've seen many aspects of our lives pulled as if by gravity into opposing camps.

Economists Steven Fazzari of Washington University in St. Louis, along with Barry Cynamon of the Federal Reserve Bank of St. Louis, conducted some research sponsored by the Institute for New Economic Thinking. They investigated the disappearance of the middle class and found a stark shift over the past decade, with the top tier progressively distancing itself from the middle. The gap grew after the Great Recession: since 2009, inflation-adjusted spending by the top earners has risen 17 percent, compared to just a 1 percent rise among the bottom 95 percent. The researchers also found that between 2009 and 2012, the top 20 percent of households, in terms of income, generated almost 90 percent of the overall increase in inflation-adjusted consumption.[1]

This economic bifurcation shows up at the local mall. Department stores that once anchored most shopping malls and focused on the broad middle market are dwindling. Consumers increasingly opt for the polar ends of the spectrum, at either dollar and discount stores or upscale boutiques and clothiers. By the beginning of 2017, the company division of TJX that encompasses discount retailers T.J. Maxx and Marshalls had experienced such a significant uptick in sales that it announced its aim to open over 800 more stores.[2] Venerable names that served the middle for generations are not faring as well; in 2017, Sears announced its intention to close 150 stores,[3] JC Penney

1   Nelson D. Schwartz, "The Middle Class Is Steadily Eroding. Just Ask the Business World," *The New York Times*, last modified February 2, 2014, https://www.nytimes.com/2014/02/03/business/the-middle-class-is-steadily-eroding-just-ask-the-business-world.html.

2   Charisse Jones, "T.J. Maxx owner could open 1,300 more stores," *USA Today*, last modified February 22, 2017, https://www.usatoday.com/story/money/2017/02/22/tj-maxx-owner-could-open-1300-more-stores/98267876/.

3   Vanessa Romo, "Sears, Kmart and Macy's Will Close More Stores in 2018," *NPR*, last modified January 5, 2018, https://www.npr.org/sections/thetwo-way/2018/01/05/575932533/sears-kmart-and-macys-will-close-more-stores-in-2018.

saw nearly the same number of closings,[4] The Limited has closed all of its locations, and Macy's announced up to 100 closings.[5]

Let's be clear: a disappearing middle is not the only source of trouble plaguing these retailers. They have suffered from a host of challenges: the terror that is Amazon, changing consumer behavior, neglect of infrastructure investments, misforecasting consumer taste, unwise financial engineering, and more. But there's no question that the hourglass economy has meant the dwindling of that big, wide fairway of the middle market that was the bread and butter of so many businesses. Upmarket brands in retail, hospitality, and consumer goods thrived—and so did the bargain ends of those categories. What suffered were the brands that had staked their claim on the middle and failed to negotiate the changing landscape.

> **What suffered were the brands that had staked their claim on the middle and failed to negotiate the changing landscape.**

For a number of years, Target was an example of a brand that had successfully navigated that changing environment and evolved with the times. They offered competitive prices on everyday goods that appealed to the thrifty alongside fashion-forward items that preserved a place on the upmarket shopping agenda. Like so many others, though, Target struggled to fend off Amazon and is now facing its own set of

---

4 Sarah Halzack, "J.C. Penney to close up to 140 stores," *Washington Post*, last modified February 24, 2017, https://www.washingtonpost.com/news/business/wp/2017/02/24/j-c-penney-to-close-up-to-140-stores/?utm_term=.8cdb7baea751.

5 Hayley Peterson, "The Limited suddenly shut down all of its stores and laid off thousands of workers," *Business Insider*, last modified January 9, 2017, http://www.businessinsider.com/the-limited-shut-down-all-its-stores-and-laid-off-4000-workers-2017-1.

issues—but let's give them credit for smartly spanning the poles for a number of years.

The disappearing middle goes beyond economic classes and retail shopping. It hardly needs to be stated that the political arena has become significantly more polarized over the past decade—just look at the rise of the Tea Party and the Freedom Caucus on one side and the Bernie Sanders phenomenon on the other. Over the past two decades, collaboration between the two parties has steadily decreased as their extreme wings became more vocal and influential, with a significant decline in the number of bills enjoying bipartisan support. Along with this trend, there was also a steady increase in the stridency of language used to describe the opposing party, moving from words describing policy differences to more fundamental critiques of character, trustworthiness, and morality.

The 2016 presidential election certainly defined new territory in terms of ditching civility for a new normal in use of language and personal attack. Love him or hate him, you do have to credit Donald Trump with tossing what used to be the accepted rules of campaigning, debating, tweeting, and pretty much every other form of communication.

"What he realized is that as a politician his job was not to *buy* media effectively," Jeff Rosenblum, Co-President of agency Questus, told me. "His job was to help companies *sell* media effectively." With news media clinging to a challenged business model and competing for a distracted audience, the ratings-worthy name-calling and barb-throwing claimed a hugely disproportionate share of airtime—again, further ratcheting up the overall emotional climate in the nation and resetting the standards for public discourse.

The media industry was itself subject to the phenomenon of polarization around a disappearing middle. While most news organizations traditionally held a certain basic orientation observable in their editorial content, they also tried to do a fair job of presenting information in a reasonably balanced manner, reserving commentary for the op-ed sections. But over the past several years, we've seen news outlets become more clearly and stridently identified with one end of the political spectrum or another, making no apparent efforts to conceal their allegiance. In fact, there's good money to be made by wearing your political orientation on your news anchors' sleeves.

Fox News is a staggeringly profitable engine within the Murdoch empire. A large part of its appeal has been its unswerving and zealous support of all things Trump, to the point where even some of its new staffers expressed discomfort at what they saw as extreme bias. CNN, which for most of its existence maintained a fairly middle-of-the-road voice, saw its rating suffer in 2014–2015. It wasn't until its increasingly confrontational clashes with candidate (and then president) Trump that it started adopting a more generally oppositional posture, at which point, guess what? Ratings rose, advertising dollars followed, and in 2017, CNN had its best year in the network's history.[6]

Not every part of the news media has had it so good. While CNN, Fox, and others were reaping the benefits of a polarizing market, local news outlets suffered. The easy—and free—availability of news and information online poses an existential crisis to quality journalism everywhere, but nowhere more so than in smaller communities. Local newspapers have been dropping like flies— just since 2008, more than 165 newspapers have either eliminated their print editions or completely shut down. Among the many sad

6   A. J. Katz, "2017 Ratings: CNN Has Its Largest Audience Ever, But Sees Prime Time Losses," TVNewser, last modified December 27, 2017, http://www.adweek.com/tvnewser/2017-rat-ings-cnn-is-down-in-prime-time-but-earns-its-largest-audience-ever-in-total-day/353147.

realities brought on by the loss of these institutions is that smaller, generally more rural communities were only able to get their news from coastal media sources. These big-city news engines felt more like alien occupiers, who didn't understand (or frankly care about) small-town America. And this helped to fuel yet another great divide in the country: between urban and rural.[7]

Big cities around the country are thriving, becoming inclusive and profitable cultural centers, while smaller communities seem to be getting left behind. On average, the larger urban centers emerged from the recent recession much more swiftly than small towns and cities. A study by the Brookings Institution's Metropolitan Policy Program compared the economics of the 100 largest communities with the 182 smallest. They found that, between 2009 and 2015, employment in the larger cities grew at almost double the rate as in the smaller ones. Income rose 50 percent more rapidly. And there does not appear to be any reason to believe that these trends will reverse themselves, suggesting a continued economic and cultural gulf between small-town and big-city America.[8]

In 2017, the Pew Research Center found that the political party divide also aligns with and reinforces the rural versus urban divide, with 65 percent of Republicans preferring large homes at a greater distance from neighbors, shops, and schools, while 61 percent of Democrats prefer to be in smaller homes closer to those amenities.[9]

7   Joe Pompeo, "The U.S. Has Lost More Than 166 Print Newspapers Since 2008," *Business Insider*, last modified July 6, 2010, http://www.businessinsider.com/the-us-has-lost-more-than-166-print-newspapers-since-2008-2010-7.

8   Eduardo Porter, "Why Big Cities Thrive, and Smaller Ones Are Being Left Behind," *The New York Times*, last modified October 10, 2017, https://www.nytimes.com/2017/10/10/business/economy/big-cities.html.

9   Drew Desilver, "How the most ideologically polarized Americans live different lives," Pew Research Center, last modified June 13, 2014, http://www.pewresearch.org/fact-tank/2014/06/13/big-houses-art-museums-and-in-laws-how-the-most-ideologically-polarized-americans-live-different-lives/.

The growing divides in economic status and political orientation, in city versus country, combine to reinforce a pervasive sense of "us against them," of embattled groups staring at their threatening opponent across an unbridgeable chasm. And when we feel threatened, we retreat into the bosom of our tribe.

RISE OF TRIBALISM

"Tribes" has become a hot word in marketing. Seth Godin wrote an excellent book called—wait for it—*Tribes,* and I highly recommend it. The idea of tribes is a powerful concept for marketers and leaders of all types—it speaks to the way in which people can rally around an idea, a value, a cause, or a leader and become energized by a resonating bond. Tribes are an inspiring idea, as they can arise around anyone who has the energy and vision to step up to lead and change the world. Everyone has the opportunity to generate the gravitational pull that creates a tribe, and there's no law of nature that limits the number of tribes that an individual may feel they belong to.

A broader sociological notion is that a tribe represents some aspect of how we think about ourselves—some characteristic or affiliation or foundation of our identity. We all have them, and we all have many of them: in my case, white, male, New Yorker, Harvard grad, diving enthusiast, soccer dad, reluctant dog owner, and so on. The strength of our affinities varies between these identities and shifts over time, depending on life-stage, evolving passions, and circumstances. Very importantly, the depth of our tribal allegiance grows dramatically when that identity is under attack.

Lilliana Mason is a political scientist and professor at University of Maryland. She prefers the term "social identity" but can live with the term "tribe." She says the notion stems from research in the 1970s that looked at the origins of World War II and the process of dehumanizing "outgroups." This is where the darker side of tribes comes in: we tend to identify most strongly with the tribal affiliation that feels threatened, she told me.

Mason cites the most recent presidential campaign as a great example of how this dynamic of threatened identities plays out. "Donald Trump leveraged this phenomenon," she said. "He pointed at groups that are not 'you' and called them responsible for your loss of status, loss of what you deserve." That aspect of voters' identity that felt most under fire also became the most salient. On the other end of the political spectrum, we saw some of the same dynamics. Bernie Sanders fueled the passions of the 99-percenters, who saw Wall Street as the source of their woes and thereby the driver of their membership in that less-privileged tribe.

> **We tend to identify most strongly with the tribal affiliation that feels threatened.**

While tribes can offer a sense of purpose and provide the framework for collective progress, they can also become the boundaries that define our separateness from others. This is particularly true when the nature of a tribal identity is inherently homogeneous. A tribal identity as a local business owner would likely put one into close contact with a set of people whose common trait is *entrepreneur*—but that group would likely represent significant diversity across age, race, gender, national background, socioeconomic strata, educational background, and more. If the part of your identity that gets activated is, say, White Male, or Wealthy 1-Percenter, you're less likely to rub shoulders with people who express diversity across other areas.

This is where we get the self-reinforcing echo-chamber phenomenon: I develop a feeling for my most salient tribal identity; through that filter I spend most of my time with people who share most of my characteristics and beliefs; I gradually dehumanize the "others" outside the tribe, who I may see as threats to my identity and who I don't understand or appreciate, because I generally don't interact with them; I choose media and "news" sources that reinforce my already-held beliefs and filter out data that does not agree with them—this sad phenomenon is called *confirmation bias.*[10]

The Tribal Echo Chamber

- develop a feeling for tribal identity
- spend time with tribe members
- dehumanize non-tribe "others"
- reinforce tribal beliefs in echo chamber
- defend tribe against perceived attack

Such a phenomenon was described in 2016 when social scientists Walter Quattrociocchi, Antonio Scala, and Cass Sunstein published a draft paper on Facebook in which they documented quantitative evidence of how social media users are likely to post content reflecting their favorite narratives, resist content they disagree with, and form polarized, like-minded groups. This, the scientists say, creates communities that rarely interact with those with opposing views, also known as "echo chambers."

When these tribal boundaries are strong enough, they become self-sustaining, as we reject the possibility that those "others" are valid human beings worthy of our time, understanding, and respect. The water cooler, the soccer sidelines, and the dinner table are no longer

---

10   Christine Emba, "Confirmed: Echo chambers exist on social media. So what do we do about them?" *Washington Post*, last modified July 14, 2016, https://www.washingtonpost.com/news/in-theory/wp/2016/07/14/confirmed-echo-chambers-exist-on-social-media-but-what-can-we-do-about-them/?utm_term=.e230837107e7.

places where people of different tribes can bridge the gaps in their understanding—each knows deep in their bones that the "other" has nothing to say that could possibly alter their point of view. And worse, each knows that any discussion might reveal or confirm that the amiable sidelines dad is actually one of "them," a supporter of unconscionable principles, a virtual enemy.

So we stay in our circles, bolster our convictions, and avoid any inputs that would uncomfortably challenge them—all of which makes us more fired up than ever to energetically defend against (or attack) those others we can't understand or respect.

NEW REALITY
TAKEAWAYS

The collapse of the middle and the rise of tribal affiliations present both new opportunities and challenges to brands. SoulCycle, for example, has done an astonishing job of creating a sense of tribe and using that dynamic to build a passionate, loyal, and profitable customer base. While it could be seen as just one more option in a sea of gym choices, SoulCycle is anything but. CEO Melanie Whelan talks of SoulCycle in spiritual terms of meditation and transformation. Its ad campaigns talk of achieving "a higher expression of yourself" and "finding your soul." The candle-lit, not-an-exercise-class has developed a cult of followers over the years that Whelan actually refers to as a "tribe." SoulCycle has successfully tapped into the craving for belonging and sense of identity that's shared across its otherwise very diverse customer base.

We'll get into more specific guidance on practical execution in later chapters. But for now, here are some questions to consider as you contemplate a more fractured, tribal marketplace:

- Do you have a clear and quantified understanding of what your brand contributes to total enterprise value?

- Do you serve a broadly defined customer base that is at risk of slipping away, as it did for Sears, J. C. Penney, Olive Garden, and so many others?

- Can you refine your value proposition to resonantly appeal to a bifurcated audience in the way that Target managed to do?

- What tribal subcultures might exist within your market?

- What aspects of your brand's DNA—your mission—might prove compelling to those subcultures, as SoulCycle does?

CHAPTER 2

FEAR AND LOATHING IN AMERICA

On January 27, 2017, President Trump announced his first immigration ban. Titled Executive Order 13769: Protecting the Nation from Foreign Terrorist Entry into the United States, the order blocked entry to the United States for Syrian refugees and, for ninety days, also banned entry for travelers from mostly Muslim countries, including Iran, Iraq, Libya, Somalia, Sudan, Syria, and Yemen. It also suspended the U.S. Refugee Admissions Program for a total of 120 days.

On January 29, 2017, Starbucks CEO Howard Schultz announced his intention to hire 10,000 refugees. A groundswell of outrage immediately broke out, with thousands protesting at Starbucks stores and on social media. Why should we give jobs to foreign citizens, the complaint went, when there are millions of us suffering here at home, facing joblessness and money worries? The inevitable #BoycottStarbucks hashtag gathered strength. Brand tracking in the months following showed a significant drop in favorability toward Starbucks.

The protesters seem to have forgotten, or didn't care, that Schultz's refugee hiring pledge followed a similar promise in 2013 to hire 10,000 American veterans. Having hit that goal a year early, Schultz increased his commitment in 2017 to set a target of 25,000 hired by 2025. The protesters' objections were driven by anxiety for their lives and livelihoods, a belief that things just aren't working for them, and a resentment of anything that seemed to prioritize unknown "others."

> "There's a pervasive feeling that the system is broken," Sarah Rabia, Global Director of Cultural Strategy for TBWA\Chiat\Day, told me. "Americans have lost trust in the people who are supposed to make it work, to fix the problems, and make society better."

As the great middle has collapsed, and we have retreated to our tribal subcultures, we have seen a parallel rise in generalized fear and mistrust. "There's a pervasive feeling that the system is broken," Sarah Rabia, Global Director of Cultural Strategy for TBWA\Chiat\Day, told me. "Americans have lost trust in the people who are supposed to make it work, to fix the problems, and make society better," she said. That fear, mistrust, and resentment add an emotional wedge to the structural and cultural divides separating us.

Social media only contributes to the velocity and visibility of all of this anxiety. Facebook, Twitter, and Instagram are easy and immediate outlets for venting angst, where it gains rapid acceleration as like-minded posters pile on and repost. One consumer's righteous indignation strikes the spark of a brand brushfire. An executive's indiscretion caught on video becomes a viral controversy. A values misstep in one branch office generates a media frenzy that swamps a CEO. This is the new reality that brands operate in, so it's worth taking a deep dive into what's at the bottom of it.

LOSS OF TRUST

The sobering truth is that we operate in an environment where the public simply doesn't trust the major institutions serving them. It doesn't trust their values, their decision-making, or their ability to get things done. It's an unfortunate reality underlying every interaction and every piece of information that consumers process, whether from politicians, the news media, or marketers.

Edelman, a PR firm, conducts annual research in the United States and around the world called the Trust Barometer. For eighteen years, the company has surveyed tens of thousands of people across dozens of countries, assessing trust levels of businesses, media, government, and NGOs. Their 2018 study revealed a deeply troubling picture: "The public's confidence in the traditional structures of American leadership is now fully undermined and has been replaced with a strong sense of fear, uncertainty, and disillusionment," according to Lisa Ross, President of Edelman's Washington, D.C., office.

The Edelman report documents what it calls a "trust crash," with every public institution seeing significant drops in trust versus the prior year. The view of businesses is gloomy, with only 48 percent of those surveyed saying they trust them to do what's right—a ten point drop from 2017's study. Trust in government was also lacking, with a dismal 33 percent expecting its officials to do the right thing.

Little surprise, then, that 59 percent of respondents also singled out the government, more than media, businesses, and NGOs, as the "most broken" of all institutions. We'll discuss later how this perception creates a vacuum that consumers expect businesses to fill. Seeing a dysfunctional government also contributes to a pervasive fear: "The uncertainty of the moment is palpable," according to Edelman's Ross. "The public is fearful."

RISE OF FEAR

When Starbucks announced a plan to hire 10,000 immigrants, they faced an immediate backlash of Americans angered by a move that seemed to prioritize foreign citizens' welfare over theirs. This reaction was fueled in part by a gnawing fear for their own economic wellbeing in world they felt had left them behind: Edelman's 2017 Trust Barometer reported 57 percent of consumers stating that "the system has failed them." And this belief provides the foundation for a pervasive fear that ratchets up the perceived stakes and emotional energy around a contentious issue.

Even our fears were subject to the forces of polarization. The 2017 Trust Barometer turned up a first-ever finding: a "Fear Gap" separating Trump and Clinton voters. According to the study, 45 percent of Clinton supporters described themselves as feeling "generally fearful," while 67 percent of Trump fans expressed the same—an almost 50 percent more widespread sense of general dread. "In this climate," according to Edelman, "people's societal and economic concerns, including globalization, the pace of innovation, and eroding social values, turn into fears, spurring the rise of populist actions now playing out in several Western-style democracies."[11]

The demons that make us fearful have changed over time, reflecting the new realities of our time. The Chapman University Survey

---

11   "2017 Edelman Trust Barometer," Edelman, https://www.edelman.com/trust2017/.

on American Fears (2017) looked at what issues keep us awake at night, and how they've changed versus the previous year. Our worst fear was Corrupt Government Officials, rising from 60 to 74 percent (remember that trust thing?). Worries about TrumpCare came in at number two. Environmental concerns cover numbers three and four. Falling off the top-ten list from the previous year are such relatively quaint fears as People I Love Becoming Seriously Ill, Identity Theft, and People I Love Dying. Taking their place are High Medical Bills, Global Warming and Climate Change, and North Korea Using Weapons.[12]

All the top worries that plague us are integrally bound up in some of the hottest, most polarizing topics of our time: government effectiveness, healthcare, foreign policy, and the environment. The issues that most divide from a policy perspective, then, are also turbocharged by nagging fears.

"All this is quite sobering," you may say, "but what does it mean to me?"

It means your job just got harder. It means that you're now expected to do more than just sell soup or soap or software. In remarks at 2017's Advertising Week in New York, Richard Edelman, CEO of the firm bearing his name, said businesses need to do more to understand and address these fears. With so little trust in a government that feels unresponsive, he said, consumers expect companies to do more to

> "All this is quite sobering," you may say, "but what does it mean to me?" It means your job just got harder.

---

12   "America's Top Fears 2017," Chapman University, https://blogs.chapman.edu/wilkinson/2017/10/11/americas-top-fears-2017/.

improve the economic and social conditions around them. If they don't step up, they risk being traded out: "Brands are something that I can control: my choice of brands can make a statement about me," he said, so a consumer's brand selection becomes their way of taking action to improve a broken world. Weighing in to support or attack a brand on the basis of its values and positions is a new form of activism, conveniently enabled and turbocharged by social media.

We'll look more at these new consumer expectations in later chapters, but we'll next examine the unfortunate new reality that gave its name to the #FakeNews Era.

#FAKENEWS

No matter whom you credit for naming it or practicing it, "fake news" has contributed mightily to the rampant mistrust and unease permeating society. Close to three quarters of Americans report being afraid of fake news being used as a weapon against them. On a global basis, 63 percent claim they can't tell the difference between good journalism and rumor or falsehoods.[13] While fake news can take many forms—real and imaginary—the very notion has the effect of making us question what we hear from pretty much every source. Sometimes fake news is just plain old bad journalism; sometimes it's solid reporting that someone just doesn't like; and now we seem to have a steady source coming from the Russians and other bad actors.

The fake news phenomenon sticks another couple of wedges in the widening societal divide. For one thing, people consuming *genuinely* fake news will likely find the support they seek for their most strident and polarized beliefs, further solidifying their positions and deepening their suspicion of the "others." For another, fake news

---

13   "2018 Edelman Trust Barometer," Edelman. https://www.edelman.com/trust-barometer.

also has an effect of generally lowering confidence in all information sources and provides an easy rationale for summarily rejecting uncomfortable points of view and stuffing virtual cotton in our ears. Trust in media has also become polarized, with 61 percent of Clinton voters expressing trust in the institution versus a mere 27 percent of Trump voters, according to the 2018 Edelman Trust Barometer.

Social media provides the perfect mechanism for adding velocity and topspin to the arguments and "data" flying around the Internet, once again raising the emotional stakes. In a world where consumers trust their peers more than businesses or advertising, social media provides a source of "news" that people feel they can believe in—it's coming from friends, right? Much has been written and said, about the role of Facebook in particular, when it comes to the outsized influence of social media on public opinion. There seems to be a meaningful effort underway at Facebook to better understand and combat the more sinister and divisive activities that we've experienced. We'll watch their progress with cautious optimism.

Even beyond its role in disseminating dubious information, social media also plays a role in raising the aggregate emotional decibel level of the content we consume, because it turns out that high-emotion rants get a lot more clicks, likes, and reposts, thereby driving more views, higher emotions, and on and on.

Researchers at Beihang University in China looked at a wide range of emotions expressed on Weibo (a Chinese micro-blogging service similar to Twitter), from happiness to disappointment, incredulousness to pride.[14] On the positive side, they found that tweets reflecting joy spread faster than those filled with sadness and

---

14   "Most Influential Emotions on Social Networks Revealed," *MIT Technology Review*, last modified September 16, 2013, https://www.technologyreview.com/s/519306/most-influential-emotions-on-social-networks-revealed/.

disgust. But the emotion that generates more momentum than any other is rage—generally from users who respond angrily to posts concerning "social problems and diplomatic issues." Aroused by this highly charged emotion, users retweet, spread the word, and pass on whatever nugget of "information" that got them so fired up.

Marketing professor Jonah Berger of the Wharton School at the University of Pennsylvania conducted a similar study, analyzing 7,000 Americans over a period of three months. Each participant was sent a series of articles from *The New York Times*, and the researchers analyzed which pieces they chose to e-mail most frequently. The key driver of e-mailing activity was not whether the article was inherently positive or negative; it was the emotional reaction the article evoked in the reader that made the difference. When readers felt sad, they withdrew and did nothing; but if the article made them angry, they become determined to gear up and do something about it—starting with sending it on to others.[15]

Let's start putting together the elements of this new reality we've been examining.

- Consumers have retreated to their tribal identities that feel most under attack.

- They are fearful and mistrustful of pretty much everything, including your company, your brand, and your CEO.

- The digital world abounds with genuinely fake news that can skew perceptions, as well as real information that readers don't trust because—you know—there's fake news out there.

---

15   Liz Rees-Jones, Katherine L. Milkman, and Jonah Berger, "The Secret to Online Success: What Makes Content Go Viral," *Scientific American*, last modified April 14, 2015, https://www.scientificamerican.com/article/the-secret-to-online-success-what-makes-content-go-viral/.

- And to top it all off, nothing spreads faster on social media than outrage.

That's where your brand lives, especially now that various forms of digital and social media have become such huge parts of our marketing agenda. And that's why today it's so easy for brands to wake up one fine morning and find themselves embroiled in a flash crisis.

> Today it's so easy for brands to wake up one fine morning and find themselves embroiled in a flash crisis.

We all know the marketing adage that one happy customer tells another person, but an unhappy customer tells ten. With the advent of social media, that math increases by orders of magnitude, as indignant and activist commenters can now reach millions with a virally appealing rant. And with the underlying fear, high emotion, and tribal echo chambers we've been discussing, brands can find themselves caught in a flash crisis brought on when an energized consumer trips the trigger.

BRANDS ON THE HOT SEAT: UNITED AIRLINES, KEURIG, ANHEUSER-BUSCH

One of the most painful instances of a brand flash crisis was the one that engulfed United Airlines in April of 2017. We all know the story by now, but in case you were meditating on a remote mountain top with no Wi-Fi, here it is: after finding themselves overbooked and needing to free up space on a plane, United gate agents were unable to entice enough passengers out of their seats with the usual inducements of free travel. Feeling out of options, the employees called on airport police to drag an unwilling passenger off the plane, bloodied and unconscious after a struggle.

Naturally, all of this was filmed by appalled fellow travelers. Powered by Twitter, the video instantly went global as consumers watched and shared in horror. Two days later, United's stock had dropped 1.1 percent, as customers all over the world posted morbidly creative memes and images of shredded United cards.[16]

In November of 2017, coffee giant Keurig, along with Realtor. com, Reddi Wip, Nature's Bounty, and Volvo Car USA, felt the swift power of the social media ecosystem. The context was senatorial candidate Roy Moore and the growing number of women accusing him of sexual misconduct. After Fox News's Sean Hannity questioned the veracity of Moore's accusers, Keurig announced that it would be pulling its advertising support from the program. Overnight, a groundswell of irate Hannity fans rose up and joined a #Boycott-Keurig movement. Many posted videos of themselves destroying their Keurig machines in imaginative ways, including demolition by golf club.

Keurig and the other ensnared brands saw the writing on the wall and quickly shifted into various manners of secondary damage control—"clarifying" their media strategy, claiming they hadn't advertised on Hannity for weeks, or blaming the announcement of pulling ads on junior staffers who "didn't understand" their policies. Keurig's CEO issued a memo to employees, apologizing for "the appearance of 'taking sides'" and promised an overhaul of internal protocols. One way or another, most shifted course under the pressure. In so doing, they managed to get out of the immediate tough spot, but

---

16   Victor Reklaitis, "United's sock falls 1.1%, wipes out $255 million off the airline's market cap," MarketWatch, last modified April 12, 2017, https://www.marketwatch.com/story/uniteds-stock-is-set-to-fall-5-and-wipe-1-billion-off-the-airlines-market-cap-2017-04-11.

PETER HORST

they didn't really win any meaningful points with either side of the issue—neither the Hannity fans nor the Hannity haters they later abandoned (more on the issue of shifting positions later).

Beyond illustrating the shocking potency of social media, this episode also illustrates another new dynamic: brand choice as social badging. With so much pent-up fear, frustration, and a feeling of powerlessness, consumers have found an easy outlet to express their ethical values and moral indignation—by attacking or celebrating brands online.

Let's face it—effecting social change is difficult work. There's lots of knocking on doors, collecting signatures, and marching in the cold. But digital activism is so much less work. Deleting an app is easy. Retweeting an irate post is easy. Smashing a coffee maker with a golf club is not only easy; it's also fun! And all the while, you feel that you've taken a moral stand *and* all your friends get to see what a principled person you are!

Now in all fairness, let's also acknowledge the great potency of social and digital media as tools of social activism to drive meaningful, positive change in awareness and attitudes as well—just as we've seen in growing focus on the issue of sexual harassment and the #MeToo movement. It's not all a story of risk and woe. The point is that consumers are primed and ready to use brands as levers in digitally empowered activism to make a mark on the world and contribute in their own small way. "I may have no hope that the government will

> **Consumers are primed and ready to use brands as levers in digitally empowered activism to make a mark on the world and contribute in their own small way.**

make any progress," they feel, "but I sure can boycott that beer or delete that app and boost my self-esteem and feel a sense of progress."

It doesn't even take a deliberate act like clubbing a customer or pulling ads from a popular news show to trigger a flash crisis. Unfortunate coincidence can also light the fuse. Anheuser-Busch started off 2017 facing a #BoycottBudweiser campaign because of their Super Bowl ad. Entitled "Born the Hard Way," the spot told the story of founder Adolphus Busch as a young immigrant journeying from Germany to pursue his American dream. By most measures, the ad was a great success: great creative quality, inspiring story, and almost 35 million views the first day, making it the most-watched ad online by that point.[17]

The ad strategy made great sense. Budweiser had seen increasing market share going to upstart craft brands, with all their gritty authenticity and relatable founders, so the brand sought to generate some of that same flesh-and-blood appeal. What better way to do that than tell the colorful, stirring (and true!) story of their own founder?

But in a miracle of bad timing, just days before the ad aired, President Trump issued his first immigration executive order banning entry into the United States from seven majority-Muslim countries. Needless to say, like most Super Bowl ads, it had been in the works for many months before the travel ban was issued and was in no way intended as a rebuttal to Trump's executive order. Regardless, the ad tripped several triggers from our hit parade of tribal fears: unknown "others," money worries, terrorism, and apparent criticism of "my president" and "my political tribe." Social media activism and #BoycottBudweiser naturally ensued. "I'm switching to PBR," announced

---

17   Tim Nudd, "The 10 Most Watched Ads on YouTube in 2017," *Adweek*, last modified December 6, 2017, http://www.adweek.com/creativity/the-10-most-watched-ads-on-youtube-in-2017/.

one irate tweeter. "DON'T take one and pass it around," exhorted another.

Budweiser wasn't the only brand to get unintentionally caught in the flash crisis following the January 27 travel ban—the much-troubled Uber also stumbled over that one. After Trump announced the executive order, several immigrants were detained at John F. Kennedy airport in New York, resulting in the New York City Taxi Workers Alliance calling a temporary halt in rides to the airport. Uber not only continued to carry passengers—some of whom were on their way to protest at JFK—but also announced a temporary suspension of their already-controversial surge pricing. Uber executives later explained that they made the move to avoid the appearance of profiting from a difficult situation. But to many, the move looked like a cynical and opportunistic attempt to break the taxi union during the strike. #BoycottUber ensued. We'll dissect this incident more thoroughly in Chapter 9.

NEW REALITY
TAKEAWAYS

Fearful and mistrustful consumers now look at your brand as a means of displaying their values and satisfying their urge for social action. With the awesome power of social media at their fingertips, their indignation can be the spark that lights a flash crisis that engulfs your brand within hours. This is a good time to ask these questions:

- What are the social/political issues you could inadvertently, unexpectedly stumble into?

- What are the corporate, product, or service policies—or lack thereof—that might cause you to trip the triggers of social outrage?

- Do you have any guardrails in place to provide decision guidance in the event that you do face a brand crisis?

- Do you have a clear process for formulating a response to a sudden brand controversy?

- Have you proactively given your customers, stakeholders, and consumers a reason to think well of you, in the event that your values and intentions are called into question?

CHAPTER 3

NO SAFE SIDELINES

"Companies have been fence-sitters, but now CEOs are being thrown into the spotlight," says Michael Maslansky, CEO of the reputation firm Maslansky + Partners. Businesses can no longer expect to be able to sit safely on the sidelines. Whereas it used to work well to say, "We don't get involved in these kinds of things," that's become a less viable position. In a world they see as broken and with a government they don't trust to fix it, 57 percent of consumers expect companies to be part of the solution, to step up to a leading role in making the world a better place, according to the Edelman Trust Barometer.

Neutrality is no longer such a safe and viable refuge. Who would have expected the NFL, the national obsession shared by virtually all tribes, to suddenly be at the epicenter of an emotionally divisive debate? But that's what happened almost overnight when players began kneeling during the national anthem to protest police treatment of African Americans. Team owners were suddenly caught in the dilemma of choosing between supporting their players' right of expression versus aligning with an angry and tweeting president—with no easy choices or risk-free solutions.

"Sports used to be a unifier, but now even sports is a divider," according to Sarah Rabia of TBWA\Chiat\Day. "Brands have to be brave in a world gone mad. If you're not brave, you risk being irrelevant," she told me. The once-safe middle ground is eroding, she stressed. "We are living in a polarized society. The Internet has given niche groups mainstream visibility, each with their own take on 'rights.' Bland, homogenous communications don't work anymore. We're more tribal and defined by our subcultures."

> We are living in a polarized society. The Internet has given niche groups mainstream visibility, each with their own take on 'rights.'

When something as broadly appealing as football becomes a political hot potato, it can be tempting to hunker down on the sidelines, out of sight. But even retreating offers no safe haven. "Every position has become politicized," Rabia said. "Even doing nothing. Silence is now considered complicity." In this chapter, we'll look at the new reality of expectations for brands to practice transparency, present themselves in an authentic manner, and choose how they will participate in (or sit out of) the dialogue around the big issues of the day.

NO PLACE TO HIDE

The reality of the digital world is that everything is out there to be sifted, examined, and judged by increasingly activist consumers. What used to be private, local, and otherwise unnoteworthy is now liable to end up being posted online and amplified for all the world to see. There's no cloak of invisibility in the digital age, and what happens in the cube farm, a satellite office, or even your backyard can become fodder for a very public brand crisis.

Just look at everyone's favorite ethical whipping boy, Uber. In the midst of a litany of other controversial issues, company founder Travis Kalanick was filmed chewing out one of his drivers during a night out on the town. The video was gleefully and virally posted and commented on, only adding to the building pressure that ultimately led to his ouster as CEO.

The CEO of KB Homes, Jeffrey Mezger, is another example of a moment of bad judgment that went from seemingly private to profoundly public when he had a few choice words for his neighbor, comedian Kathy Griffin (herself no stranger to social/political turmoil). He was caught on tape going on a potty-mouthed rant against Griffin and her boyfriend after they complained about Mezger's grandkids playing loudly in his pool. As per the new normal, the recording went viral, his bonus was slashed by 25 percent, and he was put on "double-secret probation" by his board of directors.

These brushfires also illustrate another wrinkle of our new reality: personal, corporate, and brand issues have begun to blur into one another. An executive's private actions reflect on the corporate reputation, which in turn plays a more prominent role in consumer choice at the brand level. Executive behavior and company values are no longer simply a matter for the business section of the *Wall Street Journal*—they're increasingly criteria in consumers'

> **Another wrinkle of our new reality: personal, corporate, and brand issues have begun to blur into one another.**

choices. After the Mezger-Griffin affair, for example, personal financial guru Suze Orman tweeted, "You really want to buy a home from this man? Beyond disgusting."

It's not only CEOs who have the power to spur a public reckoning with corporate values. Deep in the cubicle farm at Google, an employee wrote a memo arguing that women aren't suited to be good engineers (they're more interested in people than ideas, he opined). Despite being an internal memo, the employee's sociological musings went viral in a hurry. In the blink of an eye, Google faced a values-on-display moment and was unexpectedly put in the position of having to publicly choose between tolerating diverse opinions and enforcing its cultural tenets. In an example of successfully moving with speed and purpose, Google fired the memo's author for violating the company's stated values and beliefs.

It's not only work-related incidents that can put companies on the moral hot seat. After the Charlottesville, Virginia march organized by the alt-right in August of 2017 to protest removal of statues of Confederate generals, a photo emerged in *The New York Times* of James Alex Fields, the man charged with the second-degree murder of thirty-two-year-old Heather Heyer. In the photograph, a fellow protester from Charleston, South Carolina stood next to Fields. A resident of Charleston recognized him and called him out on social media for championing white supremacy. The photo quickly spread, as did a link to the man's Facebook page, which also listed his employer. Unexpectedly and overnight, the protester's employer fell under the glare of public scrutiny. Its Facebook page was inundated with comments about the employee's neo-Nazi ties along with negative reviews of the business. The stunned management had to scramble a response in real time, as I think I'm safe in guessing its crisis management handbook (if it even had one) did not have a section called, "What to do when an employee is photographed in a Nazi march."

And it's not only actions by company employees that can force your moral hand. Also in the Charlottesville march, tiki torches became the brand of choice for the alt-right protesters. News reports were filled with images of, and branded references to, the otherwise cheery backyard adornments. Out of the blue, the makers of tiki torches were forced to step into the social/political fray and put their values on display, likely having missed the seminar, "What to do when you're the preferred product of white supremacists." The company ended up issuing a statement distancing themselves from white supremacists and their beliefs.

The net of all these cautionary tales is this:

- stuff happens in unpredictable ways;

- everyone will know about it;

- your fundamental values will be on trial as the world watches; and

- increasingly activist consumers will display their values by taking action on your brand.

You can't stop it, but you can set yourself up to be preemptively inoculated and well-prepared to respond. More on that in Part II.

WARTS AND ALL

In a digital world where pretty much everybody knows everything, we can look at a few examples of brands that have successfully embraced and capitalized on that reality. Kim Kardashian provides a great case study in this kind of social jiu-jitsu. As far as eminent scientists have been able to determine, she's mostly famous for being famous, but that's not the point: Kardashian exemplifies key principles of the new rules of branding by living this principle: "There's no such thing as too much exposure." She has mastered the art of being inescapably everywhere, sharing the good, the bad, and the ugly with seemingly little concern for polishing the rough spots. Love her or hate her, we can learn a lot from her example.

When penning a piece for *Forbes* on these issues, I spoke with Jeetendr Sehdev—"the world's leading authority on celebrity," according to *The New York Times*, and author of the best-selling book, *The Kim Kardashian Principle: Why Shameless Sells (and How to Do It Right)*. According to Sehdev, Kim Kardashian's success exemplifies some new rules in branding that marketers should note.

"These rules are counterintuitive to traditional marketing tactics," he told me. "They include breaking molds instead of attempting to fit them, overexposing yourself as opposed to carefully crafting your image, revealing your imperfections rather than pretending you're perfect, and so on."

As succinctly articulated by the seafaring cartoon character Popeye, who declared, "I yam what I yam," this is about showing yourself to the world, warts and all. It's about avoiding the temptation to curate yourself too carefully and having the courage to show up as authentically real—and not working backwards from a market research report that tells you what people want you to be. In many ways, this principle reverses the idea drilled into every marketer's head that you need to start with the customer.

"Ideas need to be 'you-centric,' not audience-centric. CMOs need to stop guessing what their audiences want them to say and just feel free to say what *they* want to say, do what *they* want to do, and be who *they* want to be. Authenticity is key," according to Sehdev. "Playing it 'safe' in the hopes of catering to the lowest common denominator has never been a bigger risk for brands today. It's actually considered to be an act of deception, as consumers know that organizations have personal perspectives."

The Kardashian example provides an extreme reminder of a timeless brand truth: the importance of being intentional about choosing to resonate powerfully with some and bravely accepting the reality that others may not like you (or in fact may even loathe you). Kim Kardashian has clearly embraced this reality and has fearlessly bared herself (literally and figuratively) in the knowledge that those who flock to her will be passionate members of her tribe. And she seems utterly untroubled by the idea that doing so will likewise cause others to scorn and spurn her.

There's another brand that arguably practiced this Kim Kardashian principle with great success: Donald J. Trump. Throughout the campaign and well into his presidency, he resisted attempts to filter his communications or manage his persona. Most speeches were not painstakingly scripted, and he routinely shunned teleprompters. He tweeted liberally and spontaneously, used language that was well outside political and social norms, expressed opinions that were bound to offend many, and made no visible adjustments to the brand equities he'd been building over decades as real estate mogul, reality TV star, and beauty contest impresario. The price of this unfiltered display was that large segments of the nation found him detestable. The benefit was that his ardent fans would follow him anywhere: as he famously (and probably accurately) declared, "I could stand in the middle of Fifth Avenue and shoot somebody and not lose any voters."[18] I hope we don't ever find out, but I'm guessing he's right.

---

18   Steve Holland and Ginger Gibson, "Confident Trump says could 'shoot somebody' and not lose voters," Reuters, last modified January 23, 2016, https://www.reuters.com/article/us-usa-election/confident-trump-says-could-shoot-somebody-and-not-lose-voters-idUSMTZS-APEC1NFEQLYN.

DESIRE FOR AUTHENTICITY

While you might fairly question whether Kim Kardashian's "authenticity" is truly authentic, her example of shameless overexposure highlights a trend that has driven shifts in market share across many categories: the consumer desire for authenticity in the brands they choose. In many categories, from beer to snacks to fashion, much of the new growth has come from brands that display a kind of believable, flesh-and-blood genuineness. These faster-growing upstarts are the antithesis of the bloodless, antiseptic, and carefully curated corporate brands that have been losing trust and favor. They're typically smaller, often imbued with a founder's personality, and generally communicating some set of beliefs or values that will be refreshingly welcome to some, albeit potentially off-putting to others. In many cases, they very specifically celebrate or align with social issues.

In many ways the growth of these brands, with the gravitational pull of their personality, color, and values, is one more reflection of our tribal selves, clustering around products that say as much about us as they do about themselves.

SUCCESSFULLY AUTHENTIC: WILDFANG

A brand that successfully embraced the notion of focusing on a niche and its shared sensibilities is WILDFANG. Founded by two women after they left Nike, WILDFANG is a fashion brand that addresses a group they felt big-name designers had overlooked entirely: women who prefer to wear androgynous clothing. Their models are pierced, tattooed, non-gender-conforming millennials. Their tagline is "Time to raise a little hell"—but it's not raising hell just for fun. They have a strong sense of values and purpose, dedicated to designing clothing to empower women who hadn't been able to find their unique style celebrated by any other designer.

Beyond the customer empowerment designed into their product, WILDFANG engages in social causes by supporting organizations aligned with their values, for example by donating a percentage of sales to Planned Parenthood. They also waded straight into the political arena and managed to drive sales while doing it. The company posted its best results in the days right after the 2016 presidential election, powered by enthusiastic sales of their "Wild Feminist" tees and the company's own version of the recognizable red Trump campaign hat, bearing the "Make America Great Again" slogan upside down. The post-election success was not short-lived. In 2017, WILDFANG received $2.35 million in funding from venture capitalists, and the brand has experienced 80 percent year-over-year growth, with plans to open additional stores in New York City and Los Angeles in 2018.

WILDFANG illustrates another of the expectations consumers increasingly have of the brands they buy: the expectation to engage and participate in the meaningful issues of the day.

EXPECTATION TO ENGAGE

"To be silent is to be complicit," according to Richard Edelman, of the much-quoted Edelman Trust Barometer. He believes that with so much that is so wrong with the world, it's a moral imperative for organizations to step up and find a way to contribute beyond the product they sell. Keep in mind that this is not a wild-eyed activist but a guy who runs a serious, global PR shop that serves giant corporations.

Starbucks founder Howard Schultz puts it even more starkly: "Given the state of affairs, being indifferent is as evil as contributing to the vitriol, hate, and division going on in the country," he said at Advertising Week 2017. "We have an obligation to raise the level of the conversation to where it should be."

Consumers seem to largely agree. A study by the Global Strategy Group showed that 72 percent of Americans feel that companies should get involved in the discourse around important social issues.[19] Research at the Nicholson School of Communication at the University of Central Florida showed that consumers are significantly more likely to purchase brands that express opinions they agree with—and also less likely to buy brands on the other side of the issue. "People are voting with their wallets," says Lilliana Mason of University of Maryland. "They do want companies to step up and be part of the solution."[20]

NO FEAR: APPLE, STARBUCKS, AND CHICK-FIL-A

One company that has stepped into the ring is Apple, whose CEO, Tim Cook, is outspoken on everything from immigration and climate change to education and housing discrimination. Cook did not tiptoe delicately around the explosive and polarizing issue of the Charlottesville protest, strongly criticizing Trump's response to the Charlottesville violence in a staff memo: "I disagree with the president and others who believe that there is a moral equivalence between white supremacists and Nazis, and those who oppose them by standing up for human rights. Equating the two runs counter

---

19   "Americans Conflicted About Corporate Involvement in Political and Social Issues, New Study Reveals," Global Strategy Group, http://www.globalstrategygroup.com/wp-content/uploads/2013/03/3-27-13-Release_GSG-Study_Business-and-Politics_Do-They-Mix.pdf.

20   Data Freaks, "Brands Take a Stand: When Speaking Up About Controversial Issues Hurts or Helps Businesses," Forbes, last modified March 12, 2015, https://www.forbes.com/sites/datafreaks/2015/03/12/brands-take-a-stand-when-speaking-up-about-controversial-issues-hurts-or-helps-business/#2ee10554352d.

to our ideals as Americans." While he never considered himself an activist in his younger days, as a prominent leader now, he describes feeling an obligation to help make the world a better place.

True to his word, Starbucks founder Howard Schultz also stepped into the hot zone of social issues, often spurring controversy and consumer blowback. In 2013, Schultz made a pledge to hire 10,000 veterans, having been personally moved by tales of returning vets who struggled to find employment. More controversially, the company issued a similar pledge to hire 10,000 refugees in the midst of the Trump immigration policy debate, prompting the predictable #BoycottStarbucks movement.

Over the years, Starbucks has engaged in a broad range of issues, from creating affordable college options to encouraging dialogue on race relations and, of course, sustainable and responsible sourcing. Not all of these forays could be called outright successes, even in Schultz's eye, but they reflect a deeply held belief in a corporation's obligation to play a role in addressing the broader needs of society— even at the risk of generating discomfort and controversy: "You need to stand for truth and authenticity and leadership that people can believe in. Do not be indifferent."

Coming from a different end of the social/political spectrum but with a similar energy to engage is Chick-fil-A. The Georgia-based fast-food chain stirred nationwide controversy in 2015 after the founder admitted to believing in "the biblical definition of a family." The statement unsurprisingly drew energetic attention from both supporters and detractors, including a series of boycotts and gay-couple "kiss-ins." But illustrating the dynamic of clearly and power-fully appealing to a given audience (and perhaps also a testament to the addictive power of fried chicken bits), the company's revenue boomed following the controversy. Sales exploded from $6.8 billion in 2015 to almost $8 billion in just one year. Chick-fil-A expanded to the Northeast, Midwest and Pacific Northwest, and its 2,100 restaurants averaged $4.4 million in sales per unit in 2016—more than any other national restaurant chain, including McDonald's and KFC.[21]

Having survived and thrived through this controversy, and under the leadership of the founder's son, Chick-fil-A has decided to step back from engaging in purely political issues and has broadened its focus to embrace a set of community concerns beyond religion. This choice helps to illustrate the spectrum of choices companies face as they consider their posture with respect to the range of issues that may touch their brand. We'll cover those choices in Chapter 4.

NEW REALITY
TAKEAWAYS

Brands operate in an environment where their every word and action will be scrutinized and judged, as will every silence and inaction. Every piece of marketing communication from even the smallest brand in the remotest market, every action by every customer-facing employee, and every product feature will be dissected, discussed, and captured online for all eternity. With the speed of the digital news cycle, brand owners have mere hours to understand and address whatever brushfire may arise.

Adding to this volatile formula are a broad range of entities dedicated to spurring corporate action by stirring consumer passions. Media Matters of America is a progressive media watchdog group that has called out brands for advertising on Fox's Sean Hannity

---

21   Hayley Peterson, "Why Chick-fil-A's restaurants sell 4 times as much as KFC's," *Business Insider*, last modified August 1, 2017, http://www.businessinsider.com/why-chick-fil-a-is-so-successful-2017-8.

program. Advocacy groups MoveOn, Sleeping Giants, and UltraViolet gathered over a million signatures to challenge Amazon's advertising on the Breitbart website. LifeSiteNews invested in advertising to generate momentum behind its #FlushTarget campaign to protest the retailer's bathroom use policy. There's a long list of interest groups that are vigilantly seeking opportunities to rally attention and action around their cause, and brands are an excellent lever. So it's risky—verging on reckless—to assume that your brand is somehow immune to being drawn into the hot issues.

I'll delve into how to make choices in where to engage in the following chapters. But for now, here are some questions to think through:

- What brand risks might you face in terms of the words and actions of your executives and other employees?

- What can you do to present a company face that feels transparent and authentic to a consumer base that craves authenticity?

- Does your organization have a clearly articulated, thoroughly internalized policy and perspective on the issue of engaging publicly in sensitive issues?

- Do your competitors wade into broader social and political dialogue?

- What are the expectations of your key stakeholders—customers, employees, partners—for you to engage in the social/political arena?

- What are the issues that feel naturally closest to the business, its leaders, and its employees?

PART II:
NEW RULES

CHAPTER 4

IDENTIFY YOUR CORE VALUES

You're the New York area general manager of Uber when a taxi strike hits JFK Airport in response to Trump's executive order on immigration. The sudden spike in demand triggers surge pricing. *What do you do?*

You're the United Airlines gate agent of an oversold flight. You need to get some passengers off the plane, but the randomly chosen physician refuses to leave his seat. *What do you do?*

You're overseeing a cruise ship chartered to evacuate Marriott guests stranded by a hurricane. At the port are other non-Marriott vacationers clamoring to board the ship, raising questions about liability and legal red tape. *What do you do?*

You're the CEO of a Fortune 500 company, and a groundswell of employee and public sentiment rises up against you for sitting on President Trump's CEO Advisory Council, which you happen to think is good for business. *What do you do?*

While none of these are easy questions to answer, a few things are clear:

- The decision needs to be made quickly.

- There's no time for extensive discussion and debate in the executive suite.

- The world stands ready to morally judge the entire company on the basis of the decision made in that moment.

These rapid-fire dilemmas define the new normal: unpredictable, complex, no-easy-answer questions. And these quandaries are faced at every level of the organization, from front-line employees to the CEO, and in every part of the company, from the home office to a distant branch.

I wish I had the foresight to identify, document, and prescribe solutions for every possible situation your organization might face so that you could confidently avoid these social/moral flash crises. But I don't—and in all likelihood, and with great respect, you probably don't either. The answer is not in a rulebook, a policy manual, or an employee training program. All those things are of course necessary, but they're not sufficient without a crystal ball to go with them to provide specific guidance for everything you and your employees will face.

The key to navigating a fast-moving environment in a judgmental social media world is to have a clear set of values that define your culture, which in turn guides choices and actions in the moment. While this may sound shockingly obvious, it's also startling to see how often companies find themselves in hot water over an action that seems untethered to a set of values and

> **The key to navigating a fast-moving environment in a judgmental social media world is to have a clear set of values that define your culture, which in turn guides choices and actions in the moment.**

a governing culture. United's manhandling of its passenger was a painful black eye for the company. At the same time, it's hard to imagine JetBlue dragging a bloodied passenger off one of their planes, no matter how unsolvable the immediate problem appeared. JetBlue's Customer Bill of Rights and culture of bringing humanity to air travel would have made such a choice unthinkable to any employee, no matter how stressed or how many levels distant from the executive suite.

"Culture trumps strategy, every time," declared an article by Nilofer Merchant in the *Harvard Business Review*. Likewise, culture and values are the best defenses against landing in a social/moral/political firestorm. They're also the critical foundation for how you proactively set your course and navigate the tribalized, energized environment of the #FakeNews Era.[22]

IGNORE MARKETING 101 AND LOOK WITHIN

I vividly remember the first day of first-year marketing class in business school. One of the basic lessons drilled into our heads was, "You are not your customer. Always start by understanding the market, and don't inject your own ideas and sensibilities." These are wise words when it comes to designing products and building marketing campaigns. But when it comes to defining your organization's core values, you have to ignore that principle and start by looking internally. To be effective and enduring, your values need to come from a deep, introspective process that taps into the heart and soul of the organization.

---

22   Nilofer Merchant, "Culture Trumps Strategy, Every Time," *Harvard Business Review*, last modified 2011, http://www.presidentialperspectives.org/pdf/2016/2016-Chapter-8-Culture-Trumps-Strategy-Hellie.pdf.

Most companies can reach into a folder and pull out a laminated sheet entitled, "Our Values," or "Mission Statement." But the truth is that they're often pretty uninspiring, fairly interchangeable, and don't provide much of a window to the organization's soul. As often as not, these documents are written by someone in HR and approved with a cursory glance by the CEO. They tend to be filled with phrases like, "customer first" and "win in the market" and "teamwork," seemingly pulled from a grab-bag of culture Scrabble tiles.

A check-the-box approach to establishing an organization's core values will not provide the moral compass needed to guide actions in a fast-moving world. You'll end up with a default brand—that is, a brand defined by the choices made by employees in the moment, a mixed bag of marketing communications, and the myriad interpretations consumers bring in the absence of a clear understanding of your values. A default brand won't generate the kind of preemptive goodwill companies need to weather the unpredictable storms and challenges they'll likely face.

As the foundational step in equipping brands in the #FakeNews Era, defining core values requires that the senior-most leadership of the organization dig deep into the DNA of the company and go beyond the standard pablum that fills most mission and values statements. This work calls for a sincere, honest appraisal of what drives the company on many levels. Ideally, the themes provide a linkage between the very inception of the company—the reason it exists in the first place—and an inspiring vision of where it wants to go and what it seeks to accomplish.

As I said, rather than starting from the marketplace, the right beginning point here is an internal look. Depending upon the age and makeup of the company, places to look for this inspiration and grounding can include revisiting the founder's original vision (all the easier when the founder is still around); the collective beliefs and passions of the executive team; the existing culture of the broader associate base; the nature of the business itself; and the concerns of its customers.

Think of this exercise as a set of concentric circles. At the very center is the core purpose of the organization, the fundamental reason it exists. That purpose grounds everything else that follows. There are plenty of books and speeches on the subject of brand purpose, and I won't offer up yet another here. One of the best discussions of this concept is Simon Sinek's Golden Circle, where he urges organizations to start with *why*, not *what* or *how*, they do what they do. Watch him on YouTube or read his book—it's always an inspiring experience.

After the disaster of the exploding Galaxy Note 7 smartphones, Samsung was a company in deep need of a new sense of purpose and mission. Pio Schunker, EVP and Global Head of Brand Marketing at Samsung Electronics America, tells the story of seeking that inspiring North Star for the brand at an engineering-driven company. As he roamed the halls speaking with long-tenured executives, he engaged in a series of conversations with one particularly seasoned employee with deep institutional memory. This company veteran told the story of the founding of the industrial giant, decades prior, as a humble grocery store. Even all those years ago, Samsung's founder, Lee Byung-chul, was motivated by a desire to make life better for his fellow community members.

Schunker describes this insight as a revelation—the rediscovery of that original spark of inspiration to do the impossible, to accomplish what cannot be done. This bit of historical DNA provided the inspiration for a redefined organizational mission and reenergized brand, with the inspiring message: "We make what can't be made so you can do what can't be done."

I had the privilege of playing a role in the development of Capital One's first-ever mission statement. It was ultimately the product of many deep discussions, much wordsmithing, and lively debate, as everyone involved in the process brought their personal passions to the table. The final statement stayed true to the founding idea of the company—the mission to transform the credit card industry and democratize credit. Among all the other worthy mission articulations being discussed, the version ultimately chosen sprung most clearly from the vision and heart of the founder and still-CEO, Rich Fairbank. Because of the mission's deep meaning to the top guy, it became a powerful galvanizing force throughout the organization, guiding countless design decisions and investment choices.

While this introspective process needs to begin and be led from the top, be sure to make the rounds with the rank and file of the organization. They will provide a valuable reality check and diversity of perspective that will be critical in keeping yourself grounded, resonant, and honest as you develop and refine your articulation. Engaging the broader population also lays critical groundwork for the upcoming task of making sure that your purpose takes hold in the organization and becomes a part of the daily operational reality.

CHOOSE YOUR ISSUES WISELY

Once you move one circle outward from the central purpose, you start to get into the values that are essential to the organization. What are those beliefs, commitments, and principles that represent the very DNA of the organization when it's at its very best? What values are so personally, viscerally dear to leadership that they are willing to stand up for them and risk some pain?

Here it's also critical to start from within rather than looking outward to external trends and attitudes. The worst thing an organization can do is to read the prevailing winds through research and jump on a social/political bandwagon for the sake of currying favor with passionate consumers. At best, the attempt to engage will be viewed cynically, as an insincere effort to profit from the headlines. More likely, the move will generate vicious backlash, because those closest to the issue will pounce on the offending brand and lambast it in social and other media.

Perhaps the most painful example of such a transgression is the Pepsi ad featuring C-list celebrity Kendall Jenner. At this point it's almost inconceivable that you don't know the ad, but let's quickly review. A group of demonstrators gathers in the street, looking for all the world like a Black Lives Matter protest. As the group gathers critical mass, it attracts the attention of Ms. Jenner, seemingly in the midst of a photo shoot. She sheds her blond wig, wipes off her makeup, strides into the fray and marches up to the blue line of riot police, whereupon she pops open a can of Pepsi, hands it to a hunky young officer, and magically transforms the tense confrontation into a lovefest.

Now, let me stipulate that Pepsi is a great company filled with smart, well-intentioned people. And in some ways, that's the point— being smart and well-intentioned is not enough to keep you out of harm's way. But the backlash to the ad was swift and brutal. The brand was savaged from every direction, with perhaps the most devastating tweet in history coming from Martin Luther King Jr.'s daughter, Bernice King. She posted an iconic photo of the civil rights leader confronting a line of riot police, painfully similar to the scene depicted in the Pepsi ad. Her comment: "If only daddy would have known about the power of Pepsi." The ad was yanked in twenty-four hours, the CEO apologized, and changes in senior leadership were not far behind.

Figure 1

There's a critical thought process that must be employed when determining which values and issues a brand will embrace. A sweet spot of opportunity is represented by the overlap of three filters (see Figure 1). The first filter is, what matters to the world? What are the issues that are important, meaningful, and likely to improve our collective experience? Food security, clean water, confidence in young girls, gender equality, and so many more could fill this list. The second filter is, what is important and true about your brand? These may be product features or benefits, supply chain policies, community activities, and the like. The final and most critical filter is, what issues do you have permission and credibility to comment on? Where will your voice be accepted, respected, and valued? This last filter requires the most honest self-reflection. It also calls for some candid feedback from those closest to the issue who will have the courage to tell you that you may not belong in this conversation.

While I have no motivation to flog the people behind the unfortunate Pepsi-Jenner ad, it's too apt an example to not dissect it for the sake of the learning. The ad generally satisfies filter one: there is racial and social tension and strife in the world. (Although as I'll discuss later, it's not wise to latch onto a vague and broad issue versus a more focused and defined one.) The problem is that the ad missed filter two by a mile. There is no product truth that remotely connects to anything depicted in the scene (other than perhaps that policing protests is thirsty work) and certainly nothing that connects to the broader issue of race relations in the United States. Almost by definition, then, Pepsi misses filter three: they had no credibility or permission to engage in that highly charged dialogue. Yes, race relations are a critically important issue to society, but a carbonated beverage must think twice and tread carefully before stepping anywhere near the issue.

HOW FAR DO YOU GO?

As with most challenging and important questions, there is no one answer that fits every company and every situation, and I'd be foolish to try and convince you there's a cookie-cutter solution that's just right for everyone. We have companies like Starbucks and Apple that occupy one end of a choice continuum—expressing clear opinions on sharply polarizing political issues; and we have many more examples of companies at the other end, who believe they should stay completely out of the fray. As you work through your own thoughts on your brand's role, you should consider where to position yourself on this Brand Risk-Relevance Curve:

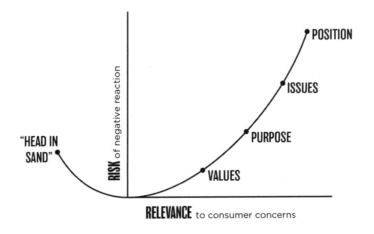

RISK of negative reaction

POSITION

ISSUES

PURPOSE

"HEAD IN SAND"

VALUES

RELEVANCE to consumer concerns

Quietly ground in **values**. Document the core values and beliefs you hold as an organization. Instill these throughout the organization as your internal moral compass. With this clarity, you can respond quickly and effectively if you're suddenly put on the spot by an unexpected firestorm. In this mode, you avoid expressing any social/political points of view outside of your core business in order to minimize the risks of blowback and controversy.

Publicly embrace **purpose**. Connect your brand to a higher-order reason for being that is larger than your brand. Over the past few years, more and more brands have been embracing purpose to add resonance and meaning to their offerings: think of Always supporting confidence in young girls; or Pampers championing happy, healthy, well-developed babies. These issues tend to be timeless, laudable, and generally uncontroversial and do not stray into more hotly debated issues.

Take on timely **issues**. Insert your brand into dialogue around more sharply defined, current issues that bring with them some inherent tension. This represents a somewhat bolder posture than embracing a broad and generally uncontroversial purpose. An example of this choice is Heineken's focus on the lack of civil dialogue between people with different opinions. The brewer waded into a high-emotion issue of the day but did not adopt a specific position.

Stake out a polar **position.** Declare yourself on one side or the other of a hotly debated issue, where there is a clear A versus B position. This is the starkest choice in terms of how to engage. Think of Microsoft declaring against Trump's immigration policy, in the full knowledge that large swathes of the nation will have strong feelings for and against the company's position. With this choice comes the upside of more ardent followership from those who agree, along with greater risk of alienating those who don't.

Having said I wouldn't declare a one-size-fits-all solution for everyone, I will say that I believe there is one posture you should definitely *not* adopt—call it **fingers in ears,** or **head in sand.** This is the inertia posture, in which you wishfully (and wrongly) believe you can quietly ride out the storm without getting touched by the swirl of issues around it. In this mode you do not even go through the work of understanding, documenting, and instilling your values and beliefs.

I hope the previous chapters have convinced you that your brand now lives in a world where you can't predict or control when and where you will be pulled into social/political debate. To be unprepared to quickly and confidently declare yourself is to embrace significant business risk—remember how large a portion of enterprise value is represented by the brand? We've seen over and over again that when your value system appears to consumers to be a blank sheet of paper, they are happy to fill in the empty space with negative assumptions based on whatever happens to be hitting the fan at that moment. This posture is Uber at the taxi strike, with consumers quite ready to believe the worst in the absence of any reason to think better of their intentions.

WHAT ARE YOU PREPARED TO DO?

From countless discussions with executives, I know there is a powerful desire to hunker down at the quiet level of **values**, steering clear of all issues that have the potential to trigger a reaction or drive a negative backlash. And for many companies, this may indeed be the right answer, given the nature of their business, stakeholders, or financial situation. But while a heads-down approach limits the risk of social/political controversy, it also raises the risk of becoming a less-relevant commodity. In a world where consumers—especially younger consumers—increasingly seek out brands whose values match theirs, entirely avoiding any expression of values or beliefs can leave you competitively vulnerable to those who have developed a more resonant connection with the market.

Many brands have leaned into a chosen purpose. Dove, along with its parent company Unilever, was an early leader in this approach with a focus on "real beauty." Countless books, gurus, and conferences abound on the subject of brand purpose, and certainly the enthusiasm for brand purpose has been valuable in many ways. It has provided resonance and energy for the brands and helped shed light on some important issues.

At the risk of sounding like a purpose naysayer, though, I will suggest that brand purpose is powerful but may not be sufficient in the #FakeNews Era. Or, said differently, you can't count on brand purpose to be your final answer on the issues your customers care about. As you look at how brands embrace purpose, particularly the larger brands that cater to a broader audience, their articulations of purpose tend to share some traits. They tend to focus on evergreen topics—timeless issues that do not represent more pressing, current tensions. They also tend to be nonpolarizing and uncontroversial in nature—who is prepared to stand up and champion the counterpoint of fake beauty, or argue that young girls should be timid and lacking in confidence? There are certainly exceptions, so please don't flood my inbox with lists of controversial purpose statements. But broadly speaking, purpose tends not to be overly risky.

But while embracing purpose is certainly a positive step, the key is to not be lured into a false sense of security that espousing brand purpose will provide a firewall against getting drawn into hotter, more controversial issues. In fact, having publicly embraced a brand purpose and its underlying beliefs and values increases the likelihood that you'll at some point need to engage—whether by choice or external pressure.

FROM PURPOSE TO POSITION: PATAGONIA

Take Patagonia, for example. What could be more evergreen, laudable, and "safe" a purpose than championing the preservation of the great outdoors and working to protect natural beauty? After years of relatively controversy-free nature loving, Patagonia witnessed President Trump sign an executive order that would dramatically reduce the acreage under the protection of national monuments in Utah. In a matter of hours, the company leapt from evergreen **purpose** to the most vocal and active **position**, taking on no less than the president of the United States.

"The President stole your land," the company declared on its website. Patagonia founder Yvon Chouinard further announced his plans to sue the president. So much for the cozy safety of brand purpose—the company is now embroiled in a public, polarizing battle with the president. This quick and bold move by the company was, at least in part, enabled by a few realities. One is that the organization enjoyed long-standing clarity about its values, its mission, and the vital issues closest to its heart. As a result, there was no need for discussion, debate, or focus-grouping when the executive order was signed. Another reality is that Chouinard, as founder of the company, has more leeway and permission than a "hired gun" CEO to take bold and controversial stances. The fact that Patagonia is a private company provides further relief from pressure against taking positions that could jeopardize short-term sales.

In Patagonia's case, the decision to step up to a stark position on a polarized issue was made intentionally by the company. It was ready and able to take advantage of that moment to both make a contribution to society and reinforce its brand's credibility and equity around its environmental positioning. But brands that wrap themselves in purpose may not have the luxury of deciding whether or not to articulate a stronger position on such an issue. Interest groups and consumers on every side of every issue have become very savvy about how to leverage media pressure on brands to spur them into vocal commitment and action. Keurig likely had no desire to engage in the politics of Alabama, but when watchdog group Media Matters called them out for advertising on Sean Hannity's program on Fox News, following Hannity's support for senatorial candidate Roy Moore, the company had to make a stark choice between remaining agnostic and appearing to support Hannity's statements versus more explicitly displaying their company values.

MEETING IN THE MIDDLE: HEINEKEN

The **issues** posture represents a midpoint between comfortable **purpose** and starkly polar **positions**. While far less common to see than brand purpose, this point on the Brand Risk-Relevance Curve represents a degree of confidence in weighing into current, pressing issues while still trying to avoid the risk of alienating 50 percent of the market. This is where Heineken went with its "Worlds Apart" campaign.

The issue Heineken took on was the lack of civil, constructive dialogue in our tribalized society. (The campaign was actually shot in the U.K., reflecting the global nature of these new realities.) They paired people with starkly opposing views on highly sensitive topics, such as gender roles, global warming, and transgender rights. Without knowing anything about each other's points of view, the pair took on a task that required cooperation and deeply personal dialogue. Upon completing the challenge, they were shown videos in which they espoused wildly opposing views and beliefs. The final challenge the pair faced was whether they wanted to leave immediately or sit, have a beer, and discuss their differing views.

Thankfully, all participants wanted to stay and talk with the person, who was now seen as a real person and not a dehumanized "other" who represented hateful beliefs. I'll go deeper into this example later on, but the campaign successfully put its finger on a troubling, present **issue** full of emotional content—but did so in a way that did not overtly endorse a polar point of view. The brand's point was that we need to talk as civil human beings (preferably over a beer), and by taking this perspective, Heineken avoided staking out a position guaranteed to offend large chunks of the population.

Position is where some brands are dragged unwillingly and where others stride confidently. In this posture, brands make statements that unambiguously advocate for one side or another of a specific and highly polarizing issue. And while taking such a position increases the likelihood of generating devoted followers who resonate with your views, it also brings the counterbalancing risk of alienating significant portions of the population. Because of this risk, most organizations—especially the large brands serving a diverse audience—will strive to stay out of this territory, seeing little but downside opportunity. But remember: it may not be up to you whether or not to stand up and declare yourself on a polarizing issue. You may be forced into it by random chance, a competitor, an employee, an interest group, legislation, or even the president of the United States.

LEADING BY EXAMPLE: CHOBANI, IBM, WINDPACT

One company that has led with its values and has not shied away from taking positions on tough issues is Chobani. Like some other examples we've mentioned, Chobani has the benefit of private ownership and an iconic founder still at the helm, so it has more license than most to wade into the fray. But founder Hamdi Ulukaya also offers sound advice for leaders pondering the risks of clearly taking controversial positions. He said recently at an industry conference that as you espouse your point of view, it's important to connect your position to the underlying reasons why you feel the way you do.

"The more you can connect your 'why' to some universal value that's driving your perspective," he said, "the more likely you are to take the energy out of the objections. The more people understand why you believe what you believe, even though they may disagree with your position, they'll respect you, because they understand why you believe it."

Even companies that don't have the benefit of a charismatic founder and private ownership make the decision to stake out positions on hotly debated and polarizing issues. IBM has energetically taken on the issue of the Trump administration's announcement that it would end the Deferred Action for Childhood Arrivals (DACA) program. This was an initiative designed to allow children who were brought illegally to the United States to stay and gain work permits. A companion initiative called the DREAM Act would provide an opportunity to earn citizenship—hence the children becoming known as "dreamers." DACA became one of the most enormously polarizing issues of the decade, ultimately leading to the shutdown of the federal government.

Amidst the debate, IBM launched a multifront campaign in support of DACA and its dreamers. The company joined in the legal effort to challenge the program's cancellation; they created stirring videos telling the stories of the IBM dreamer employees; they paraded dreamers through the halls of Congress to speak directly to legislators; CEO Ginni Rometty herself visited Congress to press the company's position. How is it that this publicly traded, Fortune 32 company invested so much energy and expense in declaring itself on this highly charged issue?

Unlike Pepsi's debatable connection to the issue of race relations, IBM has a direct and vital link to the DACA issue. The company already employs many dreamers. More broadly, the company relies on a steady stream of talented hires from diverse backgrounds and from countries around the world. The issues of immigration are vital to IBM's ability to field a globally competitive workforce, so the reality and perception of their engagement in this issue is critical to its core business. For these reasons, other technology giants like Apple, Google, Facebook, and Microsoft have also weighed in on the issue with IBM—although not all with the same level of activity and commitment.

IBM and its technology peers illustrate an important consideration when assessing whether and how aggressively to engage: How vitally connected is the issue to the fundamental business model? This connection can come in many forms, including employee considerations, supply chain issues, or concerns critical to partners and customers.

Given that these issues can be intensely personal, another avenue of authentic engagement is through the executives themselves. Howard Schultz, founder of Starbucks, speaks eloquently of the origin of his commitment to the issue of healthcare insurance: as a young child, he saw his father injured at work, rendered jobless and without any compensation or support.

On a less global scale is a company called Windpact, founded by former NFL star Shawn Springs. Windpact has developed a cutting-edge impact protection technology for sports, military, automotive and other applications. The inspiration for the company came after Springs and his children survived a catastrophic car accident without injury—thanks in part to an innovative protective lining in a child seat. That observation provided the spark for starting the company, which was further fueled by his love for the game of football and his passion for protecting the minds and bodies of those who play it. I've had the opportunity to work with the company as an advisor and consultant and have felt the broadly energizing effect of Springs's sense of purpose and personal connection to the mission.

Whether it's business or personal, the issue and the level of engagement must have an authentic and vital connection to the company or its leadership—otherwise it will be exposed as empty bandwagon-hopping and will do more harm to the brand than good.

Before you lock on your issues platform, do a thorough audit to make sure you're not sitting in a glass house. The most common ways that brands stumble around this arena is to adopt a purpose, value, or issue that they don't authentically embody or practice. When they are inevitably called out for that disconnect, the result can be excruciating and damaging—not only to your external brand but also to the morale and commitment of employees who are in the best position to see the incongruity. Do a scan through your history as a company: your products, policies, and actions in the market and the community. Look for any vulnerabilities that may crop up and create a painful contradiction between what you say and what you do.

AWKWARD IRONY: AUDI

In the 2017 Super Bowl, Audi ran a stirring ad featuring a young girl and her dad at a go-kart race. The ad made a powerful call for equal pay for women in the workplace, as the dad imagined a future in which he had to explain why his daughter earned less than her male colleagues. Watching the inspiring ad makes you want to go pick up a pitchfork and storm the gates of companies that don't provide equal opportunities for women.

Awkwardly, a great place to start might be Audi. As it turns out, they have an abysmal record of placing women in executive roles and on the board. The company therefore found itself in the uncomfortable position of having to explain its own diversity statistics in the context of its clarion call for equality. Given how long it takes to meaningfully move diversity metrics, Audi then faced the dilemma of whether to abandon the issue and appear opportunistic, or to keep up the drum beat while remaining vulnerable to criticism. So before launching headlong into your chosen issue, make sure you're fully on the right side of it.

ALL ABOARD?

Having gone through the process of aligning on whether, where, and how to engage, the last step is to ensure complete alignment and commitment within the organization. It starts at the top—leadership team, board, investors. You want to know that all parties understand, support, and commit to the values, positions, and actions that arise from this exercise. This is the time to surface any misgivings, because the last thing you want is to find yourself in the midst of a firestorm, hunkered down in a bunker with people pointing fingers at each other.

That's the position Target found itself in following a press release declaring its restroom use policy after North Carolina issued its controversial "bathroom law." The policy, which stated that customers could use whichever bathroom they felt was appropriate for them, was a long-standing Target policy and in fact was common across most of their competitors. But Target was the only retailer to issue a press release announcing that fact. A #BoycottTarget movement followed in the generally conservative state, leading to a significant revenue decline the company later attributed to the boycott. As it turns out, while there had always been full commitment to the policy itself, the strategy of calling attention to it with a press release had not been sufficiently vetted—in particular, CEO Brian Cornell reportedly had not been consulted and would not have been in favor of the announcement.

It's not only CEOs and other executives who need to be brought into the fold; at least as important is bringing the employee base onboard. This work involves not only making sure they understand the brand purpose and values but also empowering them to speak up if they see the company stray. As we'll discuss later, walking the walk carries far more weight than talking the talk. Your employees will be your first and best early warning system for ensuring that you continue on the path declared by your purpose and values.

NEW RULES
TAKEAWAYS

Consider these questions to guide you through the process of defining your core values:

- What was the gleam in the eye of the company founder? What motivated him/her to launch the business?

- What is the "why" behind what your company does every day? Why is the world better for your being here?

- What issues/values connect most vitally to your business—how you make products, who you hire, who you partner with, who you sell to?

- What issues resonate most strongly with the leadership/owners of the organization?

- Who needs to engage and align on a declaration of values and purpose?

- What is the organizational risk tolerance when it comes to the tradeoff of embracing controversy versus failing to resonate with consumer values?

- What are the downsides and benefits of taking more sharply polarized views?

- Do you have a track record of living those values? If not, can you credibly explain that disconnect and stay on a different path forward?

CHAPTER 5

UNDERSTAND YOUR TRIBE

Shortly after Donald Trump's inauguration, Under Armour founder and CEO Kevin Plank went on CNBC and declared, "To have such a pro-business president is something that is a real asset for the country."

The response was swift and, in retrospect, not surprising. A #BoycottUnderArmour movement arose amidst a swell of negative consumer response to the CEO's words. Joining in that chorus were several notable voices, including Dwayne "The Rock" Johnson and ballet dancer Misty Copeland, who both expressed strong dissent with Plank's endorsement of Trump. NBA superstar Stephen Curry put it less diplomatically when he said in an interview, "I agree with that description [of asset made by Plank], if you remove the 'et'."

What did The Rock, Curry, and Copeland all have in common?

They all had lucrative sponsorship deals with Under Armour: advertising, endorsements, branded products, the works.

The backlash from the athletes underscores the next new rule: you need to understand your tribe more deeply and intimately than ever before. You also need to think more broadly than ever about what different kinds of tribes make up your constituents. With the powerful digital megaphones at everyone's fingertips, individual voices have great reach, and they can quickly form into a unified chorus. So it becomes critically important to understand who will have a stake in, and point of view about, your brand's positions.

In Under Armour's case, it appears that when declaring support for President Trump, Plank did not fully consider a constituent group called "our sponsored athletes." Despite having no formal ties to one another, the athletes shared a stake in Under Armour's brand and reputation in the form of their own brands and career—that is, a concern for their own guilt by association. They also shared an ability to show up as a group, however spontaneous and virtual, and build critical mass with their collective influence. They were a critical constituent group whose sentiments could have been assessed, or even fairly accurately predicted, before declaring public support for a political figure or his policies.

The process of understanding your tribes starts with making sure you've identified all of them. Ranking first for most companies is *customers*. For this constituency, we have the usual segmentations and personae that we typically create: Sally the Soccer Mom, with 2.3 children, who drives a minivan, worries about saving money, uses meal kits twice a week, and so on. But while this picture of the customer helps set us up to design a product or create an ad, it doesn't provide a road map for resonating and engaging—and avoiding a brand crisis—in the highly charged #FakeNews Era.

We need to make new room in our segment profiles for a type of information we have not typically focused on when it comes to customers. We have to broaden our view beyond the data points that simply touch our product category or the more generic psychographic traits. We now need to glean such insights as: What is their political leaning? What are the social issues that motivate and concern them? How active are they with respect to those issues? Are they influencers and connectors, playing an outsized role in driving opinions and attitudes in their networks? What expectations do they have of your brand with respect to the issues they care about? Most brand owners are not accustomed to asking such questions. I suspect very few brand research managers, for example, were out in force to poll and understand the participants of either the 2017 or 2018 Women's March.

Going deeper on the concerns of customers can be another great inspiration for discovering authentic brand values and issues. Amy Emmerich is Chief Content Officer of Refinery29, a global media and entertainment company focused on celebrating women's voices and experiences. One of their partners is Planned Parenthood. Emmerich describes how Planned Parenthood found that a major concern of its client base was the challenge of reliable and affordable transportation: getting to work, going shopping, and, yes, keeping appointments at Planned Parenthood. The issue of affordable transportation then became an organically relevant issue for Planned Parenthood to take on as a part of its social/political agenda.

Increasingly, organizations have started addressing employees as critical constituents, whose needs and concerns need to be understood and addressed as thoroughly—and in fact, even more so—than customers'. This enlightened attitude has moved companies from thinking of simply providing employment to offering employee value propositions that are more than a job description and a salary. As millennials make up a growing portion of the workforce, important parts of that employment proposition are the values that drive the organization and the positions and actions it's willing to take on in social matters.

THE POWER OF YOUR PEOPLE

Indeed, employees are a powerful voice for defining brand values in the #FakeNews Era. As Trump's CEO Council quickly dissolved after the controversy over his response to the Charlottesville violence, many departing CEOs cited the enormous pressure they felt from their associates to take a values-based stand. Direct the same kind of research horsepower toward your employees as you would your customer prospects. What are the issues that motivate and energize them? What are their concerns for their lives, beyond their identity as employee? Where do they expect you to take a stand?

As the Under Armour example shows, in the #FakeNews Era we need to look more broadly at the reputation ecosystem to identify all the groups that merit attention as constituents and whose views need to be folded into our strategic thinking and tactical actions. There are many individuals, affiliations, and organizations with a strong interest in your company. And the one thing you can count on is that your every action (and inaction) will be watched, your every word (and silence) weighed, your moral fiber judged, and the resulting verdict broadcast in a public medium.

Do a thorough scan of your web of business relationships. Look through your supply chain—not just at suppliers but also at individuals or groups who have some vested interests or concerns in the process of how you source and produce your goods and services. Who are the critical partners in your ecosystem? Who is in the interconnected chain of relationships that defines the digital-age economy?

A critically important sphere to stare at is interest groups of all varieties: What are the advocacy organizations, however loosely defined, that may feel a stake in what you do and how you do it? Which groups have been active in your and related industries? Think through how your brand might provide valuable leverage in their agenda: Would this leverage be beneficial or harmful to your brand? Where is there common ground to proactively build upon, and how can you preemptively protect yourself from unwittingly becoming a pawn in their chess game?

TO UNDERSTAND, GO BEYOND THE NUMBERS

Modern marketing has provided a wealth of powerful tools for gathering data and analyzing market trends, and these can be put to great use as you try to more deeply understand your customers and influencers. But it's important to remember the limitations of these technologies, especially when it comes to the nuanced business of generating insights into motivations, emotions, and aspirations.

The history of marketing—and probably life itself—represents a continual swing of a pendulum: We develop a great new capability that captures our imagination with all its possibilities; we overuse that new toy until we drive consumers insane and do damage to our brands; and then we bring some common sense back into the equation and moderate—and sometimes overly moderate—our use of that great new capability.

I've seen this across many industries. The wonder of direct mail, and its ability to confidently target messages and track results, led us to carpet-bomb American mailboxes to the point of massive consumer frustration and eroding brand equities. It's easy to measure the positive value of that fraction who respond to the solicitation, but it's much harder to track the negative effect of poisoning the brand with all those annoyed nonresponders. Likewise, the advent of scanner data in the consumer packaged goods industry provided a wonderful new source of insights around consumer purchase drivers. Manufacturers gleefully promoted, couponed, and priced their brands into commodity oblivion. And we've all experienced the joy of digital ad retargeting: the ability to track an individual's browsing and slap them with repeated messages to push them over the edge to purchase—unless we push them over the edge of insanity, because they already bought the shoes, or decided not to, or had lent the computer to their grandmother and never really needed orthopedic mall-walkers in the first place.

We're at a point where I see looming the same exuberant overuse of new marketing technologies. Big data, algorithms, high-powered analytics, automation, artificial intelligence, programmatic media—the list goes on. All are critical, powerful new tools that modern marketing leaders must understand and incorporate in appropriate ways. But as always, there's a great temptation to lean too heavily on these technologies and decide we don't have to think so hard any more. After all, who can argue with the output of a massively sophisticated hunk of engineering?

In the enthusiasm for the proliferating bells and whistles, it's become high fashion to heap scorn on qualitative, nonnumeric insights. Just try to find one of the cool kids talking about what they learned at a great focus group or a revealing, in-depth interview. What we need to remember is that when it comes to the subtle, interpretive business of understanding human emotions and motivations, we can't just abdicate that work to the machines. Extracting truly catalyzing insights from the marketplace still requires a curious, creative, human thinker—looking at the data, certainly, but also looking more broadly, at the social and cultural context. It's a relatively simple task for a machine to correlate purchases of taco chips with a host of other variables, but it takes a human to go deep into consumers' mind-set to understand what will cause them to get energized, join a cause, or boycott your brand.

As cultural strategy expert Sarah Rabia told me, "There's still a role for good old-fashioned qualitative insights, spending real time with consumers, taking a macro view of culture." She calls on marketers to get out of the "coastal bubbles" and immerse themselves in the lives of the people they seek to serve. "You need to spend time with real people, to relate and connect with them," she said.

A kindred spirit is Christian Madsbjerg, a partner with the consultancy ReD Associates. He wrote the book *Sensemaking*, and it's well worth reading. In the book, Madsbjerg argues passionately that we face great risks in overreliance on algorithms, tech, and analytics. He calls for a more humanistic, liberal arts approach to balance all the technology and for marketers to immerse themselves in the cultural context to yield more powerful and actionable insights.

In an interview with *Forbes*, Madsbjerg cites a project he conducted to examine credit card fraud—an area where banks and other financials devote extraordinary analytical and technical horsepower. Taking a more anthropological approach, his team spent time with fraudsters to understand how they think and what motivates them as they conduct their nefarious business. He pointed to two examples where the humanistic approach unearthed insights that the data gurus missed. Madsbjerg's team discovered that the fraudsters often stocked illicit "stores" of their swindled goods, which meant that they typically bought the same items in many sizes. The researchers also learned that fraudsters sought to create distance between their daily "regular" lives and their felonious occupation, so they would typically send their purchases to remote or empty buildings. Feeding both of these cultural insights back into the analytic process significantly increased the bank's ability to spot and prevent fraud.

So how do you operationalize this kind of immersive, cultural-insights philosophy? Madsbjerg offers these steps:

Focus on thick data—not just the thin data. Don't just spend time on the sterile facts and figures. Look at the broader context of the consumers' lives, their pains, their wishes.

Visit the savanna—not the zoo. Leave the bubble of your office, don't study the report from inside the vacuum of headquarters. Immerse yourself in your consumer's life, walk in their shoes, sit in their living room, hear the emotion in their voice.

Think creatively—not operationally. Abductive thinking is nonlinear problem-solving, and it's the only way to get truly breakthrough insights. Start with an educated guess and apply it to the data without demanding rigorous logic behind it, and then follow the winding road of the insights.

Follow the North Star—not the GPS. Develop a feel for the market, its rhythms and pulses. Allow yourself permission to rely on your deep understanding and genuine caring about the product and its users. Leverage expertise, judgment, and instinct every bit as much as data.

An interesting thing will happen as you and your colleagues spend time walking in the shoes and living the daily lives of your consumers: you'll develop a more powerful empathy and visceral passion for what matters to them. There's just something more infectious and energizing about experiencing another's truth versus simply consuming the facts of it intellectually. As I discussed earlier, so much of a company's success or failure in this arena comes down to the authenticity of its words and actions: Is this simply an ad designed to capitalize on market research, or is it a genuine expression of conviction and commitment to a belief? A great way to build an authentic fire in the belly (especially among office-bound executives) is to provide them with the opportunity to have that multisensory experience of truly living in their consumers' world. With that shared experience and common passion, the follow-through will be more genuine, consistent, and convincing.

As you're doing this immersive, anthropological delving into your consumers' lives, remember to keep your radar tuned for their various tribal affiliations. As we discussed earlier, a consumer's sense of tribal identity will be a powerful catalyst to their thinking and their actions. As Andrew Sullivan wrote in his *New York Magazine* article, "America Wasn't Built for Humans," "One of the great attractions of tribalism is that you don't actually have to think very much. All you need to know on any given subject is which side you're on." This short-circuiting of the process of evaluating information and deciding on a position means that consumers will be that much more knee-jerk in their responses. Keep a sharp eye open for which sense of tribal identity is most likely to feel under siege—as that is likely the one that will be most powerfully felt and the most likely to motivate action.

GET THE RIGHT PEOPLE AT THE TABLE

"Keep your friends close, and your enemies closer." So said Michael Corleone. Or Machiavelli. Or Sun Tzu. There's some debate on the matter. In any case, the #FakeNews Era corollary is, "Keep your tribes close." By now, you've laid the foundation of articulating your purpose, defined your core values and beliefs, gone deep on understanding your consumers and their values, and identified those tribes that will play a role in your brand's health and reputation. The key now is to stay close to those groups and enroll them in keeping you honest and effective.

Regardless of where and how you engage, there will inevitably be nuances, considerations, and perspectives that you will not fully understand and appreciate. That's not a condemnation of your enlightenment or caring, but it's a reality that we are all prisoners of our own experiences. There's a natural limit to how comprehensively we can see and understand all the hot buttons, facets, and sensitivities of highly emotional issues. The opportunity to miss one of those nuances and step on a landmine is ever-present—even with all the goodwill in the world.

I was recently conducting one-on-one interviews at a technology company where I was doing some consulting on culture and purpose. One of the other participants was an up-and-coming young African American professional in the sales organization. In the course of sharing our experiences, he described a no-win challenge he faced every day. A major cultural tenet of the organization was to energetically embrace conflict with passion. This naturally soft-spoken executive said, "I'm a six-foot four-inch black dude—if I really get into it with someone, there's a good chance that will be really scary to them. So, do I embody the culture and run the risk of frightening them, or do I tone it down and know that I'll be dinged in my year-end review for not being passionate? I feel that tension every day."

As much as I liked to think of myself as someone who tried to bring empathy and awareness to my surroundings, this daily tension the sales executive described was not one that would likely have occurred to me. As obvious as it seemed in retrospect, the only way I could ever learn of and appreciate this dilemma, and the gnawing no-win inescapability of it, would be to hear about it from the lips of the guy feeling it every day. Now, if this were an issue that somehow was factoring into a marketing or communication agenda, you can imagine all the ways in which I might have unintentionally sparked an enormously negative reaction in the marketplace.

As you embark on a values-based agenda and engage in issues beyond your product category, make sure you bring the right people into the room. Make it a standard, no-exceptions process to solicit feedback from people closest to whatever issue you're addressing—and make sure you listen and hear with giant ears. They will surely see facets of the topic that escaped you, yet were strikingly obvious and important to them.

> **As you embark on a values-based agenda and engage in issues beyond your product category, make sure you bring the right people into the room.**

There are many ways to create this feedback-rich environment, and you should do all of them. The first and overwhelmingly most important action, of course, is to make sure your internal staff demographics reflect the reality of your marketplace. A roomful of white, forty-something men will surely stub their toes trying to market to a diverse millennial audience, let alone trying to engage authentically and effectively on social and political matters. This is a huge and critical topic well beyond the scope of this book, but I'd be criminally remiss by not starting the importance of a diverse workforce.

Even a well-diversified staff is not enough to protect yourself from ham-handed missteps. There are too many issues, too many considerations, and too many tribal subcultures to have them all adequately hardwired into your organization. Look at those tribes you identified as constituents and influencers and reach out to them. Find ways to develop ongoing relationships. Invite them into your thought process. Share your goals and beliefs and make your good intentions clear. Get their input on your plans and tactics and absorb the feedback without being defensive. Pay particular attention to language. There are subtle nuances and major implications in the shades of word choice.

> **There are subtle nuances and major implications in the shades of word choice.**

Naturally, one positive outcome of reaching out to these groups and individuals is that you'll enroll them as supporters and believers—critically valuable if you should ever stumble and require a supportive, third-party voice. By opening up and exposing your values and intentions, you stand the chance of earning an advocate in the court of public opinion, should you ever find yourself on trial for a social/tribal/political infraction.

After the Pepsi/Kendall Jenner debacle, a common question amidst all the withering criticism was, "Who was in the room when this was written? Or produced? Or shipped for broadcast? Who said this was OK?!" It seemed clear after the fact that Pepsi was likely missing a critical voice in the discussion leading up to the airing of the offending ad. Whether that voice wasn't present, wasn't empowered, or wasn't heard is unknown to us on the outside. What is clear is that the process lacked the porosity to absorb the sensibilities and sensitivities necessary to take on the weighty issue of race relations—or to decide whether to address the issue in the first place.

When discussing the topic of values-driven branding, it's hard not to reference Dove. For years now, the Dove brand has pretty much been the poster child for embracing purpose at the heart and soul of a brand. Dove has generated acclaim, awards, and more than a few misty eyes through their campaigns championing "real beauty" in the face of so many advertised images of idealized, unachievable female perfection.

It was all the more sobering, then, to see that even a brand and company so energized around purpose could stumble so badly. A three-second GIF for Dove body wash was posted to the brand's Facebook page in the fall of 2017. The brief video, with the headline, "Ready for a Dove shower?" showed an African American woman pulling off her brown shirt to reveal a white woman underneath. That woman in turn pulled her white shirt off to reveal a third woman wearing a beige shirt, who had a vaguely Hispanic appearance. She then pulled her shirt off to reveal an Asian woman.

One can imagine a well-intentioned brand manager or social media specialist thinking that this ad was a great way to celebrate diversity and show that Dove embraces people of every race and ethnicity. And yet those good intentions were not enough to protect the brand from the quick and stern response.

"How can you see a body wash ad like this and not realize? It rubbed me and many people the wrong way," said Naomi Blake, a beauty industry entrepreneur and social influencer.[23] Black Girl Culture, with the Twitter handle @blkgrlculture and over 57,000 followers, wrote, "Dove is just following in the footsteps of past soap companies who use white supremacy to promote their products," and posted images of decades-old soap ads showing black children scrubbing themselves to reveal white skin underneath.

---

23 Jackie Wattles, "Dove apologizes for ad: We 'missed the mark' representing black women," CNN Money, last modified October 9, 2017, http://money.cnn.com/2017/10/08/news/companies/dove-apology-racist-ad/index.html.

In fairness to Unilever, the many posts and articles criticizing the ad focused on the first two images—the black woman seeming to peel away her skin to become white. Zeroing in on that 1.5-second segment created a very different impression, for some viewers, than seeing the entire mini-story play out. Blogger @StrangePintura, with close to 20,000 followers, pointed this out, conducting her own mini-poll that showed a more positive response to the entire message.

But brands don't get to choose how the public consumes and critiques their work. Unilever quickly pulled the ad and posted a thorough and sincere-sounding apology. It seems clear that the motivations, values, and intentions of the Dove team were not the issue—the problem is that the right eyes were likely not on the piece before it went out, so no one in the production chain perceived what would be so obvious to so many others.

The Dove misstep illustrates one of the great challenges where modern marketing meets the #FakeNews Era. The offending Dove ad was a three-second piece of video—one small tidbit of creative output among thousands of other Dove-branded marketing bits sent out into the universe. Modern marketing calls for a near-constant stream of content created by decentralized, agile teams operating with great speed and autonomy. A lifetime ago, earlier in my career, I used to have a simple rule of thumb for my team for approving marketing materials: "I see it before the consumer does." That was practical in the quaint and simple days before the digital revolution. But in a modern marketing ecosystem, with dispersed teams generating content and responding in real time to social signals, no such critical-path review is feasible by a manager—let alone by a group of tribe-sensitive advisors.

NEW RULES
TAKEAWAYS

The imperative then becomes to instill as much of that sensitivity and awareness into the people around you as possible. Leaders must continually reinforce the brand's values and purpose in words and, much more importantly, in actions. Employees must see decisions made and costs incurred by management on the altar of values and purpose. They must be empowered and encouraged to ring a virtual bell when they see the organization drifting from its stated values. Diversity of staffing must be a mandate for the C-suite, the board, and the broader organization, with bonuses dependent on progress. Relationships must be formed and nurtured with outside groups and influencers who can provide perspective, coaching, and support in the line of fire. This last point is especially critical, because along with death and taxes, you can pretty well count on someone calling you out in public in the #FakeNews Era.

Ask yourself these questions as you go deep on understanding your tribe:

- Look broadly at your business ecosystem: What are all the different groups that make up your tribes—your constituents?

- Develop a deeper, richer understanding of your customers, going beyond the usual segmentation scheme data: What are their hot-button issues? What might get them to #boycott you?

- Look particularly closely at your employees: What are the social and political concerns that particularly motivate them? How might they expect you to engage with those issues?

- How can you go beyond sterile data and start getting immersed in the lives of your customers, walking in their shoes, and understanding their daily cultural reality?

- What interest groups and influencers are likely to raise their voices around your industry or your brand? What is their agenda? How might they use you for leverage? How might you engage them proactively for input, guidance, and support?

- Does your organization appropriately mirror the marketplace? Do you have the diversity of perspective you need to communicate thoughtfully and sensitively to a tribal consumer market?

CHAPTER 6

PUT YOUR VALUES ON DISPLAY

Finch Knitting and Sewing Studio, on a quiet corner in Leesburg, Virginia, sells supplies and holds regular classes for people interested in knitting and sewing. It's a small business in a small town, catering to a small group of local enthusiasts. The shop shares little in common with mega-brands like Budweiser, Apple, Nordstrom, or Uber. It has essentially zero brand awareness. It isn't run by an iconic business titan with controversial views. It doesn't produce big, splashy ad campaigns, sponsor major celebrities, or really do anything that you'd think would garner meaningful notoriety.

What does it share in common with some of those giant global brands? It ended up in the crosshairs of tribal conflict in the #FakeNews Era.

"We are compiling a list of local Leesburg businesses that are openly hostile to customers who voted for Donald Trump," stated an e-mail to Finch owner Nicole Morganthau. The e-mail's author, a "Michelle Morgan," claimed to have received a tip about Morganthau posting anti-Trump sentiments in social media and threatened to put Finch Studio on a boycott list if the owner didn't respond quickly and satisfactorily.

Morganthau was indeed a frequent user of social media on behalf of the business. She produced a regular stream of cheerful, colorful posts on the joys of knitting and upcoming events at the store. What she didn't do was use that outlet as a political soapbox. The closest thing to a polarizing message was a perky post about having pink yarn for sale the day before the Women's March on Washington in case anyone wanted to knit any pink hats—hardly a controversial political rant.

When it came to her own personal social media accounts, however, Morganthau was more forthright about her own political leanings, favoring the Democratic agenda. In this way, her experience highlights one of the realities of the #FakeNews Era we discussed earlier—what is personal is now business. There is no longer a firewall between an executive's personal brand and their business brand, between one employee's action and the company's assumed policies. With ready consumer access to digital information and interest groups' time, resources, and motivation, you can expect to be called out for what you do outside the office context—even if you're not the famous founder of a disruptive tech company.

Morganthau's experience also illustrates another reality of this hyper-politicized environment: even small, low-profile businesses are subject to the passions and politics that have vexed the giant brands. While so much of this drama plays out on the national stage, politics and social movements are still inherently local in many respects. It would therefore be a mistake to assume that being a smaller business with a modest marketing budget offers any immunity to the new realities. Large brands, small businesses, and everything in between face the same challenges in the #FakeNews Era.

On a more encouraging note, the Finch Studio experience also illustrates another critically important lesson on how to successfully navigate these choppy waters. Morganthau did not capitulate to the threatening e-mail but rather stuck to the values that her business stood for: inclusiveness and openness to anyone and everyone with a passion for knitting and sewing. She responded, "The Finch family is a safe haven, a neutral space where any and all beliefs are sacred and anybody should feel welcome. All belong here." She posted the correspondence on her social channels and the issue gained significant regional attention, with local TV channels picking up the story.

> Large brands, small businesses, and everything in between face the same challenges in the #FakeNews Era.

FIRST, WALK THE WALK

Morganthau's response was more than just empty words in the moment of crisis. It represented the values underlying the Finch Studio and the way that she and her colleagues served their constituents. She wasn't just talking the talk—she had spent years walking the walk. The proof of this was in the response she received, with locals rising to Finch's defense. "Oh for crying out loud," read one supportive post. "I suppose this is all political because you welcome ALL! Good grief!" Another Facebook post declared, "I don't knit or crochet but you and your store is [sic] really making me rethink that decision."

Having consistently lived the values of inclusiveness and openness in its everyday business operation, Finch was able to weather the storm of threats and boycott lists—and perhaps even win over a few non-knitters. They walked the walk and put in place the most effective protection against the threat of getting sucked in the social/political swirl: preventative goodwill.

As we get into some guidelines for execution, let's break down what "walking the walk" means here:

- You have total clarity on your brand values and beliefs.

- All employees clearly understand and embrace the brand's values and beliefs.

- You consistently exemplify those values in the choices and actions taken in the course of operations.

- Your marketing and communications are harmonious with those values and beliefs.

Notice the order of operations here: Think, Do, Say. The words are, of course, important, and we'll spend some time on that later. But the words are more effective when they follow actions—and they're nowhere near as powerful as the actions. And it all needs to be grounded in values and beliefs that you've thoroughly thought through.

As you go through that thought process, here are some questions to ask yourself:

- Given the business category you operate in, which issues are naturally the most relevant?

- What are the profound beliefs of the founder, the leadership, and the associates?

- Is this a large brand with broad reach and diverse concerns, or a niche brand with a focused following with shared interests?

- What are the concerns and risk profile of the owners and other stakeholders?

- Ultimately, what is the business prepared to stand up for in the face of dissenting opinions and threats?

The process of assessing values is not a fast one, according to Paul Argenti, a reputation expert and professor of corporate communication at Dartmouth's Tuck School of Business. "It's time-consuming," he told me, "and most companies don't have a clear set of well-articulated values, nothing that is differentiated in guiding action. Most companies don't have any kind of process for defining values."

Once defined, it's critical to make sure that every employee understands and can recite the values. Argenti cited former GE CEO Jeff Immelt as spending the better part of a year traveling the world and meeting with employees to talk about company values, both refining their articulation and at the same time instilling them in the rank and file. This is the critical, hard work that must be done at the outset—otherwise you'll bob like a cork over the various conflicting tides and forces that will act on your brand and drive actions and decisions by employees in the moment.

I spent twelve years at Capital One, which, for a guy who spent years hopping across industries, is a good, long stretch. A big reason for that long tenure was the company's values—and I know this was also true for many others.

When you spend any amount of time at Capital One, you can't help but get a very clear feeling for its values. Even when you interview for a job at Capital One, you'll likely get to know their values long before you get a job offer. It's inevitable that someone on your schedule will pull out a copy of the values statement and refer to them, either sharing an anecdote or explaining how much they mean to him or her personally. And you can be sure that the final hiring assessment will require a firm belief that the candidate will embrace and support the values.

Capital One's values implicitly underlie most every conversation, and they are also explicitly referenced on a regular basis. As a litmus test for decisions, they offer a way of assessing whether a strategy, a product design, or a communication lives up to the headline principles of *Excellence* and *Do the Right Thing*. In addition to those top-line statements, the values drill down to address a broad array of principles around decision-making, the customer, strategy, and more. Perhaps most importantly, the values are a critical North Star for company culture and a yardstick for assessing individual performance: "Lives the values" is a part of everyone's annual performance review.

Why are the company values so alive and so frequently on employees' minds at Capital One, when so many companies pay mere lip service to theirs? It's because they represent the deeply held convictions of the founder, chairman, and CEO Rich Fairbank. Capital One's values are a window into what he believes are essential for an ethical, winning company.

Let's face it, values statements at many companies are the result of an HR-led process that results in nice-sounding words, which then get reviewed and blessed by someone at the top. As often as not, those values then live somewhere on the internal website, in employee onboarding materials, and ... not much else. As a result, they don't mean much and don't drive much thinking, decision-making, or action.

But the values statement of Capital One wasn't the output of an HR gnome's to-do list: it was carefully, painstakingly crafted with the intense involvement of Fairbank. Each and every word was carefully chosen to deliver maximum—sometimes multiple—meaning. The very process of drafting them was an example of living the values, with Fairbank insisting on personally working on them until they fully met his standard of excellence, with unusual and powerful combinations of language such as, "Share information, time, and credit."

With that kind of visceral commitment and resonance at the top of the company, there was no way the values could be anything but the vital heart of its culture. With so much energy invested in the expression of what *Excellence* and *Do the Right Thing* mean, it was inevitable that everyone in the company would rise to the challenge of delivering on those values every day.

EVERYONE SHOULD BE THE BRAND MANAGER

Most of us at one point or another have said, "Relax, we're not curing cancer here." Well, at St. Jude's Children's Hospital, they are. It's an extraordinary organization that provides medical care for children with all forms of cancer, and they do it without ever presenting a bill to the parents—not for doctors' fees, hospital costs, tests, or anything else related to treating the child. They also provide for the housing, feeding, and even transportation of the patients' families—because their core belief, and the heart of their brand promise, is that "All the family should worry about is helping their child live." I suspect you'll agree with me that this is one of the most compelling articulations of a brand ever written: it clarifies the entire—and unique—purpose of the organization; it taps into a powerful, universal emotion; and it makes you wish you could work there.

St. Jude's didn't leave it at that. In order to make sure that energizing brand statement was truly baked into the everyday operations of the organization, every single employee has a brand goal in their annual performance review. Not just the people in the marketing department but absolutely everyone is held responsible for doing their part for building the health of the brand.

You can imagine the howls that might arise if you were to implement this plan at most organizations: "What can I possibly do in accounting/IT/finance/HR to influence a brand metric?!" the aggrieved employees would wail. And yet imagine the creative thinking and new perspectives that would be sparked by such a move: how to write loan rejection letters in a way that actually builds the brand; how to make receiving an overdue bill notice a positive experience; how to reduce back-office paperwork so that customer-facing employees can more readily deliver a cheerful experience.

NOW, TALK THE TALK

With alignment across leadership and the rank and file, and with the whole organization walking the walk, we can now look at the business of marketing and communications. We all know how hard it is to get the public to remember that our detergent cleans dishes brighter, or that our credit card offers double rewards, or that our audit services can handle the most sophisticated problems. Grabbing even a small piece of mindshare requires consistency, time, and relentless focus. Just look at one of my favorite brands, Geico, and see how unswervingly they've focused on driving home the message, "15 minutes could save you 15 percent or more on your car insurance."

It's even harder to convince the public of your values and beliefs.

It's more difficult for a few reasons. Remember that atmosphere of skepticism and mistrust we talked about in Chapter 2? That doesn't help. Most brands aren't starting from a position of strength and credibility when it comes to establishing their moral *bona fides*.

We're also talking about concepts that are frequently less tangible and less amenable to convincing proof points like, "Has twelve essential vitamins!" or "Now with xylitol!" So building up the protective layer of goodwill and belief in your values will take more than just a passing effort from the community relations team or the ad agency. It will require that you get all of your activities aligned and working together to maintain a continuous and consistent drumbeat.

As you take on the challenge of putting your values on display, think *radical transparency*. Let's face it—everything you do and say is sitting somewhere ready to be discovered, so be radically and pro-actively transparent in the interest of allowing the world to see and believe what's in your heart. You should be all the more confident in doing so after getting the entire organization onboard. Look for all the opportunities to share the big and small ways that you're living up to your stated values. Create venues for sharing at multiple levels, from the corporate initiative to the actions of individuals on the front lines. Find hero stories, create internal lore, and celebrate them externally.

A consistent complaint I've heard at just about every company I've ever worked at is, "We do all this great work in the community, and our brand just doesn't seem to get credit for it." Most organizations have a lot of ways they engage with their communities and their causes, between donations, employee volunteer programs, sponsorships, and other forms of support. And when all is said and done, the employees feel inspired, recipients are grateful, and good work is done—but the broader world doesn't seem to appreciate or even know about all that good work, making less impact on the overall brand that the organization would hope.

The problem tends to be one of focus. Community engagement at many organizations is generally a bit ad hoc—some is driven by corporate priorities, some arises from local requests, and some are executive interests. As a result, the organization's roster of good works is a mixed bag of people and issues and places, and it doesn't add up to a critical mass and a coherent proof of commitment to a focused set of belief, issues, and values. The problem with focus is that it calls for sacrifice—that is, what will you *not* do? Who will you say "no" to? How will you reallocate your funds and energy to better align to a tighter set of issues and causes that play a supportive role to your overall brand purpose and values?

Despite the difficulties of doing a reset like this, there are several benefits to this kind of focus beyond achieving the critical mass that will lift your efforts over the attention threshold. One benefit is that you will build up a more extensive and consistent track record of actions that align with your promise—walking the walk. Another important benefit of this focus is that if you find yourself in the hot seat, with your brand on trial in the court of public opinion, there will be that many more witnesses ready to testify on your behalf about the very values that you are likely defending. So a disciplined alignment of your community activities not only builds your brand equities but also builds up protective goodwill against the day when you face the glare of public judgment.

BAKING YOUR VALUES INTO YOUR CORE MARKETING: FRITO-LAY

In September of 2016, just as election frenzy was reaching a peak, Frito-Lay introduced what was possibly the worst product in the history of consumer packaged goods: a bag of Doritos with no flavors, no crunch, and more specifically … no chips. The offering was a part of the company's partnership with Rock the Vote, an initiative to get younger Americans to register to vote, following the dismal 38 percent turnout among that population in 2012. Digital vending machines asked would-be consumers if they had registered to vote. Those who pressed "NO" were presented with a bag of faux chips they didn't choose, along with a message informing them that when you don't vote, you likewise don't get a choice. The chastened munchers were then given the opportunity to begin the process of registering to vote right on the vending machine's digital screen.

Doritos' "Boldest Choice" campaign was just one of many efforts that represent a sustained commitment on PepsiCo division Frito-Lay's part to operate at the level of **issue** engagement, per the Brand Risk-Relevance Curve we described in Chapter 4. Frito-Lay CMO Jennifer Saenz has been leading the charge on these values-based marketing efforts. She and her brands offer a useful beacon for how to engage with difficult issues—all while building and protecting the brand.

Saenz started by grounding herself in the new realities facing her company. "If you're a brand that wants to have a dialogue and be noticed by consumers," she told me, "you have to be involved with culture. You have to be involved with what consumers are interested in. They want to know there are shared values, and they look to the world to help define their identity."

Saenz said Frito-Lay began exploring and engaging with issues of deeper social and political import because they're relevant to the brands' audiences. "We took that on with Doritos initially because those kinds of issues were especially relevant to its target—younger millennials and Gen Z, who tend to be more purpose-oriented and more thoughtful about many of these issues," she told me. The company also used the Stacy's brand to support women's issues via the "Stacy's Stands with You" campaign. The brand produced nine special-edition bags, each inspired by a sign carried at a rally or by a pivotal moment in the history of the women's movement.

Going beyond mere voicing of support, Stacy's also offered up free bags of chips and promised donations to Step Up, an organization that provides mentoring to young girls. And stepping even further into the action, Stacy's chip bags also contained Snapchat codes that directly called congressional representatives during women's marches and rallies.

Both the Doritos "Boldest Choice" and "Stacy's Stands with You" programs are great examples of a brand moving beyond the relatively safe zone of timeless **purpose** and stepping into more timely **issues** that have a greater potential to stir controversy and negative response. And both of the programs provided clear and tangible opportunities for consumers to take action and make an immediate contribution to improving the problem, through money or personal engagement.

Saenz says this is the zone they strive for in their social engagement—to take on real, current challenges and issues but to deliberately avoid going as far as taking a polar **position** on a hotly controversial topic: "We try to get to a place where it's a meaningful issue but that taps into a universal feeling and where hopefully people on all sides would say, 'Yeah, this is how it should be,'" she said. "With Stacy's, we want to support women exercising their voices and being heard," Saenz told me. "Whatever that issue is. We try to understand the common ground across groups that is consistent with the core values of the brand but leave the debate point to consumers to have a dialogue with each other."

While many brands have gotten on the purpose train, Saenz agrees that today brands need to dive in more deeply than broad purpose. As an example, the company launched Doritos Rainbows in September of 2015. These were Doritos chips in five bright colors with the tagline, "There's nothing bolder than being yourself." They were a part of a program to support the It Gets Better Project, an effort to address suicide risk among LGBTQ teens. Consumers could get the colorful chips by making an online donation of at least $10 at ItGetsBetter.org. The product sold out in days, raising $100,000 for the organization and generating a large dose of media attention.

"We looked at the issue of teen suicide as a 'Who could argue with it?' kind of issue," Saenz told me. "But we also knew that there was a high likelihood that we were going to get negative commentary about a very divisive conversation."

Sure enough, Doritos experienced all the usual moves out of the standard playbook: outrage on social media, calls for a boycott, angry communications to the home office. "You just lost my business. I'm sick of having this shoved in my face from every direction," tweeted one irate consumer. "Congrats. You just lost a lot of people. Way to go … Doritos are no longer allowed in my home. Idiots," fumed another.

The good news, though, is that Saenz and her colleagues had laid the groundwork to prepare the organization for that potential reaction. "We always take a thoughtful approach," Saenz said. "We always start by checking in with consumers to make sure that what we're thinking of resonates with them. And when taking on social issues, we engage with PR, government affairs, legal, and often third parties to get their perspectives—to help us anticipate reactions and think it through." When a brand is leaning into an issue that the team feels has the potential to generate a controversial reaction, Saenz told me they do run the program up the corporate flagpole to ensure visibility and alignment before proceeding.

No matter how much pre-work is done, though, Saenz says there is often an unexpected reaction. "The programs where we've chosen to engage, we take a point of view that is consistent with PepsiCo values—inclusion, women's issues, engagement in communities," she said. "So we haven't had to back off under the pressure. We accept that there are people who don't share our values, and we're happy to defend against whatever might happen from those who disagree."

NEW RULES
TAKEAWAYS

Here's the key message: With grounding in deep-seated corporate values, alignment among key internal stakeholders, and input and guidance from the relevant communities to find the resonant tone, a brand can lean confidently into a meaningful issue. That legwork allows the team to stay the course and avoid the ping-ponging around an issue on the basis of the loudest detractor or most recent call to the CEO's office.

Here are some questions to consider as you begin to execute values-based marketing:

- Have you been intentional, thoughtful, and realistic about where on the Brand Risk-Relevance Curve you want to land: **values**, **purpose**, **issues**, or **position**?

- Are you taking on an issue that flows directly from the core purpose and values at the heart of your organization?

- Have you secured the right level of internal visibility and buy-in (CEO, operating executives, board, PR, legal) based on the level of potential risk?

- Does your program offer meaningful contributions to the conversation and not simply a vague endorsement?

- Do you provide consumers with clear and tangible ways to become a part of the solution themselves?

- Have you anticipated the potential reactions to the program and thought through your response?

CHAPTER 7

NEW RULES IN ACTION— HEINEKEN'S "WORLDS APART"

Now that we've gone through the considerations and pitfalls to watch for when navigating a brand through the current treacherous environment, let's stop and take a close look at one example. I'm a big believer in going deep on the anatomy of others' work—you can learn a ton by really staring at it and obsessing over how it functions. The learning can be equally powerful whether it's a beacon of success or a cautionary tale of woe. This is where curious marketing minds are so valuable—teasing apart the elements, obvious and subtle, that work together to make a piece of marketing powerful and compelling versus ho-hum and forgettable.

Heineken's "Worlds Apart" campaign provides a ton of learning, so we'll spend some time here on it. I won't call it perfect, but I think it's an ambitious and great piece of work. Others disagree, and we'll come back to their arguments in the next chapter. And while the work generated goodwill for the brand, even Heineken leadership questions whether it was entirely the right direction. If you haven't seen it, I encourage you to check it out—it's easy to find on YouTube, and you'll find it thought-provoking, whether you love it or hate it.

Here's the premise: Heineken introduces us to several pairs of individuals who express wildly divergent points of view on some of the hottest and most polarizing issues of the day. One declares that a woman's place is in the home, while his counterpart describes herself as "100 percent feminist." Another says that "a man is a man" and all this transgender talk is nonsense, while his counterpart is in fact a transgender veteran. One calls climate change bunk, while the other calls it a critical threat. Without having seen one another's videos, the polar opposite pairs are thrown together in a giant warehouse, unaware of their violently contrasting worldviews, and given a series of instructions to complete a project.

Without any clear idea of what their goal is, the two have to collaborate to interpret the instructions and build a structure that remains unclear. At a midpoint, they're told to stop the work and ask each other a set of introspective questions—leading one to remark how much they have gotten to know about each other, despite so little time together.

The collaborative construction continues until it's clear they've built a bar. At this point, the pair is directed to watch the videos that they had previously recorded. We're able to see the shock on their faces as they learn of the abhorrent beliefs held by their project partner—and new friend.

The final challenge put to the pairs is a choice: they can go home, or they can sit down at the bar they've built and have a chat over a beer (Heineken, of course).

The anti-transgender chap did in fact stalk off the set—only to quickly return with a smile and say, "Got you!" Each pair in fact opted to sit and talk, and we get to see bits of their dialogue. I'll admit I found this to be a goosebumps moment, as several opened up to share what lay behind their beliefs and expressed openness to the other's views. (Remember Chobani's Hamdi Ulukaya talking about how people will respect you as a person for *why* you believe something, even if they disagree with your position?) What was most moving is that after their shared experience and personal exchanges, they saw their partner as a whole human being—not simply as an embodiment of a hated opinion. By collaborating on the project and exchanging intimate thoughts about who they are and what drives them, their tribal defenses were disarmed, they were able to have a civil dialogue about difficult issues, and—maybe, just maybe—open their minds a bit.

Going back to the Brand Risk-Relevance Curve, Heineken here has opted for issues—jumping into a sharper, more timely debate than a broad and timeless purpose but stopping short of specifically coming down on one side of a polar question. While one could certainly make a safe guess as to which of the partners Heineken likely sympathized with, their focus was not to convince the world that *"climate change is real."* The agenda was clearly to shine a light on our inability to conduct civilized dialogue in a polarized society and to call for a more positive and constructive discourse across tribal boundaries.

"Worlds Apart" offers a good primer in how to engage positively and sure-footedly in challenging issues. As I said, the work is not immune to criticism, and we'll look at some of the

What Heineken got right, and you can too:

1. Pick a focused issue
2. Choose an appropriate aspiration
3. Find a genuine role for your brand
4. Be authentic, not polished
5. Walk the walk

weaker points. But let's start by focusing on what Heineken got right in seeking to take on a tough topic. And with no malice toward the people of PepsiCo, we'll contrast "Worlds Apart" with Pepsi's Kendall Jenner ad for the sake of clarity.

Pick a focused issue

Heineken set its sights on the issue of civil dialogue. It's clear, simple, and real. It's also a pretty universal issue—no matter which end of which spectrum you occupy, you can probably nod your head and agree that we're simply not listening to each other and that the volume of the debate has gotten too high. Between the echo chambers of Twitter and Facebook communities, the bias-confirming polarized media, and the generalized angst of the day, we're all just stuck in the ruts of our thinking, and we're shouting louder than we're listening. That's a genuine, focused problem, and Heineken steps on no landmines by calling it out.

By way of contrast, the context for the Pepsi/Jenner spot was a vague, undefined scene of conflict—one marcher held up a sign with the pointedly un-pointed slogan, "Join the conversation." More problematically, the scene looked remarkably like a Black Lives Matter protest, which opened the brand up to scorching criticism for co-opting that deadly serious issue. It's not totally clear what problem they seemed to want to solve, and they strayed into places they did not have permission to enter.

Choose an appropriate aspiration

Heineken's objective was as simple as its problem statement: We need to talk to each other like people. They didn't presume to solve world hunger, end the battle of the sexes, or alter the pace of climate change. Their aspiration was clear, valuable, and achievable: Let's start a dialogue. Let's dial back the emotional energy, try to believe that the "others" are not necessarily monsters, and open our minds to constructive conversation. By taking on a meaningful but reasonable goal, Heineken invites us to believe in their sincerity and perhaps even their commitment to it (more on that later).

An overly ambitious goal—like, say, transforming a near-riot into a lovefest with the police—invites scorn. By showing Kendall Jenner instantly turning the tides and bringing about societal harmony, Pepsi appeared to trivialize the underlying problems and demonstrate a lack of serious intent to make a genuine contribution.

Find a genuine role for your brand

As with many of these purpose- and values-driven campaigns, the brand takes a backseat—a reason why many companies object to investing in these programs. "Worlds Apart" is no exception—but despite its short time on screen, the brand plays an appropriate role for the storyline and for the campaign's message. At the pivotal moment, the participants can choose to leave or to discuss their views over a beer. That's what you do in real life—you crack open a beer and have a chat with friends.

In this work, I think Heineken found a sweet spot for its product's role. It was not a distant, peripheral piece of window dressing that contributes nothing to the story. At the same time, it did not somehow claim that a bottle o' suds could catalyze major changes in social relations. In this story, a beer does what a beer does, and Heineken didn't pretend it could do more.

In the magic hands of Kendall Jenner, however, the simple pop of a can of Pepsi was able to melt a tough cop's heart and bring sunshine and happiness in the midst of urban strife. In case you weren't sure, bubbly sugar water does not actually end riots, and the mere implication was maddening to many.

Be authentic, not polished

The people featured in "Worlds Apart" have the look and feel of real people. They're colorful and engaging, but they're not polished, prettified, and poised. Depending on your point of view, you'll likely think they're righteous or ignorant, but you still have a sense of genuine human beings expressing themselves with candor—with no obvious attempt to smooth over the rough edges that all real people have. The "realness" of the participants makes us more open to believing that Heineken means what it says.

We talked earlier about the pervasive desire for authenticity—so much so that "authentic" is on the verge of becoming an overused and thereby less useful term for marketers. Consumers generally, and millennials particularly, crave a level of authentic connection to the brands that play a meaningful role in their lives. Especially when engaging with an issue of social/political/emotional importance, it's critical for a brand to show up as sincere, genuine, and believable. In her own particular way, Kim Kardashian built her brand with a "Here I am, with all my flaws and no apologies" authenticity that continues to fascinate and enrapture her followers.

How ironic then that her sister Kendall provides a perfect contrast to Heineken's real people, with layer upon layer of phoniness in the Pepsi ad: the carefully curated ethnic diversity of the protesters, complete with an Asian cello player practicing his etudes in the middle of the chaos; the presence of the C-list celebrity with no perceptible connection to any issue of social importance; the hunky, Chippendales-looking riot cop. At every turn, the unfortunate spot feels contrived, a surface-level dalliance with matters of life and death.

Walk the walk

Consumers are savvy, cynical, and suspicious when it comes to brands, and they will quickly sniff out a statement of values, belief, or purpose that lives only in a glitzy ad campaign. As in life, words matter, but actions matter more. Heineken showed through its actions that it was committed to the issues of civil dialogue beyond an online video. It wasn't a one-off campaign that lived only on TV, as with Audi and their ad about equal pay for women. Heineken invested in a multifaceted set of initiatives focused on bringing people together.

Heineken worked with Facebook to develop a chat bot that brings together people with different points of view. They sponsored a research program led by Goldsmiths, University of London on the science of common ground. The company also partnered with the Human Library, a not-for-profit that uses conversation to challenge stereotypes. Heineken has shown commitment with their dollars and their energy to this issue of bridging the gaps between people with divergent beliefs.

In our last flog of the Kendall Jenner dead horse, it's not clear what, if any, actions Pepsi took to actually champion social harmony outside of its investment in a splashy TV ad. And with that, I promise not to mention the beleaguered ad again.

Heineken has done a nice job of stepping bravely into a very real, very challenging issue and taking a thoughtful, credible, and seemingly sincere approach to helping us all make some progress. In doing so, the brand has illustrated some important principles for a successful effort.

Keep in mind

1. Tie back to what's unique about your brand
2. Watch for subtle but powerful sensitivities
3. Enable consumers to walk the walk

At the same time, in the spirit of "nothing is perfect," let's take a look at some of the points where the spot missed the mark.

Tie back to what's unique about your brand

In all brand positioning and marketing, the objective should be to connect your promise to something special and unique about your offer in order to lift your brand above the competitive fray. It could be a tangibly differentiated feature, a patented technology, a cost advantage, or an edge in quality. Sometimes it's more conceptual or emotional, such as perception of exclusivity or luxury or a distinctive personality.

A less ideal approach is to leverage a more generic category trait and try to take ownership of it by striking first or by executing more effectively than the competition. There are certainly great examples of the generic category strategy working brilliantly. Folgers sold millions of pounds of coffee on the promise of "the best part of waking up"— that great smell of a cup of fresh-brewed java. Now the last time I checked, most coffee smells pretty good when you brew it, so that's about as generic a category truth as you can get. To try and make it more proprietary, the brand also declared a proof point of "mountain grown." Not all coffee is grown on mountains, but a whole lot of it is, so that too is far from a unique selling point. But Folgers executed against the category truth brilliantly and consistently, so they effectively seized that trait as their own.

Under the heading of shamelessly learning and stealing from success, I pulled a similar strategy while managing Pop Secret Popcorn, as a bright-eyed youngster. After a technology patent expired and competition matched our product quality, I turned to that uniquely alluring buttery aroma as the category truth I would grab as the foundation of my positioning and brought that trait to life in advertising.

In "Worlds Apart," Heineken found an *appropriate* role for its brand—we all sit around and have a chat over a beer. What they didn't find is a *unique* role for its brand. You can have a chat over any beer—there's nothing special about Heineken that makes it uniquely well-suited to fostering candid dialogue. Most every brand of beer, not to mention a bottle of wine, iced tea, or even fresh-baked cookies, can also serve as an accompaniment to a good chin wag. Heineken has no proprietary hold over beer chats, and this spot isn't likely to confer it. In the realm of communicating your brand values and addressing issues, you probably do have more room to take this generic approach, but a strategy that connects to some ownable truth will ultimately deliver more brand value.

Watch for subtle but powerful sensitivities

Earlier we discussed the importance of getting a 360 view of your work through diverse eyes in order to avoid any unintended stumbles over sensitive issues. While "Worlds Apart" does seem to take a generally sensitive approach to the people representing the polar points of view, they may have missed at least one concern. As I have spoken on this topic and shared the Heineken spot around the country, I have heard a number of women express a strong emotional reaction that I would not have anticipated. They shared a distressed empathy for the feminist who was paired with a male counterpart who declared that "feminism today is man hating" and that men need women to have their children. They could vividly imagine how they would feel if they'd been put in a position to unknowingly spend time with someone who felt that way. On behalf of the female participant, they felt angry at Heineken for subjecting her to what they considered an ambush. While my anecdotal findings of indignation on behalf of the participant may not hold up on a broad statistical basis, the concern may have been worth a closer look and a defter touch.

Enable consumers to walk the walk

Heineken put its money where its mouth was by investing in a number of programs to further the agenda of civil dialogue. What they didn't do was provide a clear path for consumers to engage and become part of the solution themselves. Frito-Lay, on the other hand, offered a vehicle for action by enabling phone calls through codes on chip bags and by helping people register to vote at a vending machine. The more that you can facilitate consumers engaging and taking action, the more good things will happen. For one, the direct link between your brand and the consumer's actions will strengthen your brand's association with the issue. For another, by virtue of taking action themselves, consumers will confer more positive equity on the brand than if they had simply thought positive thoughts on their couch. And perhaps most importantly, you'll increase the odds of actually making a positive contribution to the very issue you're taking on.

NEW RULES
TAKEAWAYS

As you refine your approaches and study beacons in the marketplace, here are some questions to ask yourself:

- Do you have a tight, clear definition of our issue that will immediately resonate with our audience?

- Does your brand have permission—and sufficiently insightful guidance—to wade into this issue?

- Are you setting a goal that is meaningful, bold, and yet reasonable—e.g., seeking to feed 10,000 families next year but not proposing to solve world hunger overnight?

- Does your brand play a role that is sensible, believable, and—ideally—unique to your brand? If you're attaching to a category truth, what can you do to take more proprietary ownership of it?

- Have you rigorously scrubbed the work for signs of artifice and contrivance and enabled a genuine commitment to show through?

- How can you provide avenues for consumers to play a meaningful role in furthering the cause that you're supporting with this work?

- Do you have a clear road map for how your actions will support the message?

PART III:
LEADING UNDER FIRE

CHAPTER 8

OVERCOMING INTERNAL OBJECTIONS

I've always been a big believer in the power of the devil's advocate to improve your thinking. By taking the opposing view of whatever position you're ready to adopt, you challenge your thinking, pick apart your logic, and poke at all the weak points of your argument. By doing so, one of two things happens: you wind up changing your mind, or you refine and improve your position to make it even stronger. That's why I've always tried hard to cultivate an open culture in all of my teams, so we could ensure that all the best thinking was on the table and subjected to rigorous interrogation, and I wasn't just breathing my own exhaust as the leader.

In that spirit, then, let's spend some time on the opposite side of the argument I've been developing these past chapters around engaging in the broader issues facing society. We'll call this the, "Hey, we're running a business, not a charity" argument. This rationale says that Heineken should sell beer, not constructive dialogue, and Starbucks should sell coffee, not refugee empowerment. Using corporate resources to support anything but growth in sales and profit is to stray from the definition of your role and from the very purpose of the business in the first place, the argument goes.

There are several reasons why we should spend some time with this point of view.

IT'S A FAIR POINT

Unless your company's owners have clearly stated their desire to invest in a social/political agenda, it's quite fair to ask whether resources should be devoted to anything but profit. We've certainly seen a number of examples of brand purpose run amok, seeming to overwhelm any commercial agenda. In a world where few companies are seeing the kind of growth that makes boards smile, it's not unreasonable to suggest that all hands should be on deck to improve sales—not society.

YOUR BOSS AND YOUR BOARD ARE LIKELY TO SAY IT

Not every organization is led by executives with great passion and commitment for engaging in issues beyond their product, as Starbucks, Apple, Chobani, and many more are. In fact, most companies do not start with such energy and a mission at the top, so if you aspire to take on bigger issues, you can expect to hear questions and challenges about how such initiatives relate to the bottom line.

YOU'LL SHARPEN YOUR THINKING

Winston Churchill reportedly said, "True genius resides in the capacity for evaluation of uncertain, hazardous and conflicting information." More recently, Roger Martin's fantastic book, *The Opposable*

Mind, looks at the power of embracing conflicting points of view and considering disparate possibilities. So, wherever you end up, you'll be better off by challenging yourself with the opposing point of view.

Let's put on the devil's advocate hat, then, and walk around some of the reasonable and predictable arguments against engaging in broader social/political dialogue. After a fair hearing of the objections, we'll circle back to weigh those points of view in the broader context of the new realities for marketing in the #FakeNews Era.

We'll begin with the most straightforward and obvious objection:

Possible Objections to Entering the Fray:

1. You're in the business of selling beer/chips/cars/tax software/cloud computing—not social change!

2. There's no upside—and we'll offend 50 percent of the market!

3. Consumers are savvy and cynical—they won't believe us

You're in the business of selling beer/chips/cars/ tax software/cloud computing—not social change!

Hard to argue with, right? What's the last time you met an organization that got paid well to champion a social cause, or fight for an underdog, or shine a light on uncomfortable truths? Isn't the definition of business "creating and keeping customers"? What does that have to do with world hunger, gender equality, or immigration policy? There are many individuals and organizations with clear charters to take on those issues: Why on earth should a pizza company sign up for social causes when there are fierce competitors battling each other to provide a hungry public with innovative wheels of flour and cheese?

Mark Ritson is an eloquent proponent of this point of view. If you're not familiar with him, I encourage you to spend a little time reading some of his columns or checking out his talks on YouTube. He's a professor of marketing at Melbourne University and a prolific writer on all things brand and marketing. I find his perspectives to be very sharp and generally delivered with a great sense of humor and a delight in sticking a thumb in the eye of the cool trends of the day—such as obsession with millennials or over-exuberance for all the whiz-bang analytic/digital/targeting toys.

He's also particularly critical of brands investing energy and resources in purpose, or politics and social causes. Ritson recently observed in *Marketing Week* that "the reason marketers are employed is to make money for the companies that employ them. Preferably lots of it." Ritson believes there should be a bright line that distinguishes the professional work of building a business and driving profits from the decision to engage in more altruistic, social-minded activities in one's personal time.[24]

Ritson sees the rush of brands embracing purpose as a result of sloppy thinking by marketers and a sheepish discomfort at the notion of focusing solely on profits. How much better it feels, he says, to produce films about environmental risk than to market boring commercial widgets. Commerce is grubby; purpose is cool. Ritson also cites the work of Richard Shotton, Deputy Head of Evidence with the advertising firm MG OMD, in which Shotton debunks the arguments and data that sought to show that brand purpose drives greater profits.

---

24 Mark Ritson, "Mark Ritson: Heineken should remember marketing is about profit, not purpose," Marketing Week, last modified May 10, 2017, https://www.marketingweek.com/2017/05/10/heineken-marketing-purpose-profit/.

For those reasons, Ritson is not a fan of the Heineken "Worlds Apart" campaign: "I think it's crap. Absolute crap."

While he acknowledges that the campaign was well-produced and raised important issues worthy of discussion, he believes it also represents misspent resources. To begin with, Ritson points out the issue of generic brand linkage that we discussed in the previous chapter: Sure, it's a real thing to sit and have a chat over a beer, but that's no more true of Heineken than Budweiser, St. Pauli Girl, or any other brew. Add to that the low-key branding of the spot, and you have only a passing impression of beer and discussion—not likely to drive a massive spike in near-term sales.

Ritson grants that "Worlds Apart" would likely do no harm to the Heineken brand. But that's not a high enough bar, he argues:

> Just because a campaign does no harm, or perhaps a little good, does not make it a success. There is the important issue of opportunity cost to contend with, and what Heineken could have done with the money. What would have been the outcome had Heineken invested the money, time, and other resources they ploughed into world peace and mutual understanding into selling a bit of beer with a strongly branded campaign for Heineken instead?

The opportunity cost argument is certainly a fair one: I've not yet met the marketer who felt over-flush with funding, and who struggled to find ways to deploy an ample budget. Modern marketing has become a continuous exercise in assessing what's working and making painful trade-off decisions across investments—often between those likely to drive short-term sales versus longer-term equity.

With the reality of a low-growth economy and shareholders breathing down your neck, can you justify investing even a penny in any initiative that strays from the focused path of driving sales? Even if you're not outright hurting the brand with a ham-handed misstep, you're incurring the opportunity cost of a more single-minded commercial campaign, right?

This is likely the first and most fundamental argument you'll hear as you contemplate whether and how to weigh in, and because it is a fair point of view, you will sharpen and strengthen your thinking and conviction by fully addressing it.

> **The question of why to spend on a values-based campaign goes back to my very first recommendation: dig deep into your core and assess what beliefs, values, and sense of mission exist—or don't exist—within the organization and its leaders.**

First and foremost, how you answer this question goes back to my very first recommendation: dig deep into your core and assess what beliefs, values, and sense of mission exist—or don't exist—within the organization and its leaders. It may well be that there is no visceral energy to engage your brand beyond product sales and into broader issues. Or perhaps there are strong beliefs, but there isn't sufficient conviction that those beliefs can be productively harnessed for any commercial benefit. The task then becomes articulating that connection and convincing the stakeholders that a sincere commitment to those convictions deserves some place—big or small, public or internal—in the brand's agenda. This argument is won only partially with numbers and logic; rather, it is primarily made with passion, conviction, and vision.

This question of whether broader social purpose offers commercial value also goes to the heart of what is so wonderfully, frustratingly challenging about marketing: the need to wed art with science, judgment with data, vision with pragmatism, and short-term sales with long-term brand. Certainly, analytics and quantitative thinking are important drivers of modern marketing, especially as the state of the art in marketing technology begins to do a better job of assessing more strategic issues like brand equity. But there remains the important role of good, sound judgment, whereby smart leaders need to wrestle with the question of whether a "safer" focus on tomorrow's sales will lead to regret down the road at not having forged a more meaningful bond with the market. Factors to consider include not only the immediate and obviously measurable effects on next quarter's sales—there are also the following:

- the growing demographic and economic cohort of younger consumers who have clearly stated they want to engage with brands whose values match their own;

- the recruiting, retention, and inspiration value of a workplace that values more than just selling widgets;

- the likely improved regard among regulators, legislators, and other influencers; and

- the goodwill in the bank that can be drawn upon in the event of a brand crisis.

I can't offer a crisp formula for weighting these factors in an equation, but I can encourage you to make sure that you give them full consideration as you debate and determine your brand's role in the larger world.

I can also point out one person who thinks businesses do need to make a difference beyond simply making a profit. His name is Larry

Fink, and he runs the $6 trillion asset management firm Blackrock. You could say that Larry Fink essentially *is* Wall Street and represents the voice of those who are most concerned with a steady and growing stream of profits from public companies.

In a letter he sent to CEOs around the world in January of 2018, Fink declared that governments are failing in their duty to address the major challenges that loom in the future: "As a result, society is increasingly turning to the private sector and asking that companies respond to broader societal challenges." Fink explicitly pointed to purpose as a critical North Star to guide corporate decisions: "Without a sense of purpose, no company, either public or private, can achieve its full potential. It will ultimately lose the license to operate from key stakeholders." He cites environmental impact, workforce diversity, community engagement, and employee retraining as among the larger issues companies must grapple with.

Needless to say, this is a fairly surprising point of view to hear from the guy charged with delivering returns on trillions of dollars of invested capital. But it is also both permission and challenge to go beyond a mere focus on profits to also play a role in making the world better.

There's no upside—and we'll offend 50 percent of the market!

Here's another fair and reasonable challenge. We all know what a wildly polarized environment we operate in, with hair-trigger tempers accompanying the opposing viewpoints. For a brand of any scale that lacks the luxury of a niche customer base committed to the same values, choosing a side means almost certainly alienating a large part of the marketplace. The calculus can get scary: it's easy to envision the drop in sales from disagreeing prospects and harder to count on the potential lift from those who agree with you.

Proponents of this viewpoint abound. They include reputation experts, pollsters, and marketing leaders. And they're not wrong. Every statement of a polar position comes with a measurable lift among agreers and a corresponding ding from disagreers—with the scale and relativity of those movements varying by issue, by brand, and by consumer segment.

This objection, though, presumes that a brand has made the decision to stake out a **position**—that fourth and highest level on the Brand Risk-Relevance Curve. In this place, a brand has selected a specific and polarizing issue that calls for a yes/no, for/against answer and has declared a specific point of view on that issue—for example, Microsoft supporting same-sex marriage, or Starbucks opposing Trump's immigration policy. It's predictable that a large portion—if not close to half—of the country will find those positions objectionable. This way of engaging certainly brings with it the highest-octane risk/reward profile: the greatest likelihood of energetic support from some and violent rejection by others. This decision relies most heavily on hard-to-quantify factors like employee engagement, long-term franchise value, and a desire to be on what you believe is the right side of history.

But to declare a polarizing **position** is just one of the ways a brand can engage. It's a false choice to say a brand must either go all the way out on the limb of a hotly debated, A versus B issue or opt to remain in a vacuum, sealed off from society. At a minimum, all brands and organizations should ground themselves in the **values** they believe in. They may also consider whether to elevate their posture and their voice into **purpose** or **issues** engagement, which doesn't bring with it the daunting risk of alienating a large portion of the marketplace. Again, resist the urge to oversimplify the problem and overly narrow the available choices: the question is not whether to go starkly political or remain inert. You have a range of ways in which to make your brand vital and relevant before you get to the place of choosing sides.

Consumers are savvy and cynical— they won't believe us

Here's another very fair and real concern that is borne out in the numbers. Research conducted by Ipsos Connect showed that as brands rush to publicly embrace purpose in their marketing, consumers can become frustrated and mistrustful at what they see as poorly fitting, self-serving social initiatives. Already suspicious of brands and advertising to begin with, consumers look at the earnest and lofty purpose campaigns with increased cynicism when they are not preceded—or at least quickly followed—by real action in the real world. Unfortunately, even committed brands that do walk their walk can find the well poisoned by the bandwagon-jumping opportunists whose intentions don't extend beyond a thirty-second ad.[25]

With all the concern around stirring controversy and alienating consumers, why then would you risk all that if consumers are just going to doubt what you say and, even worse, think poorly of you for being another one of those "arrogant," purpose-spouting brands?

The answer to this takes me back to a time, ages ago, when a well-intentioned boss was lecturing me with extensive instructions on all the ways I must be sure not to screw up an initiative I was launching. I mustered every ounce of patience I had in me as I smiled

---

25   Omar Oakes, "Prove your brand purpose or consumers won't believe it, warns Trinity Mirror," *PR Week*, last modified June 29, 2017, https://www.prweek.com/article/1438053/prove-brand-purpose-consumers-wont-believe-it-warns-trinity-mirror.

and nodded dutifully at this windy string of obvious don't-dos. But I couldn't stop myself from responding with, "Thanks for that coaching. I'll sure try not to be an absolute moron."

In many ways, that's also the answer here, too. Yes, consumers have grown cynical from watching brands make thin attempts at winning favor with passing waves at big issues. And yes, the bar is high for communicating values and purpose in a convincing manner to a suspicious consumer. So ... don't be insincere and opportunistic. Start with a grounding in what you believe in and care about—and if the answer is "nothing much," well then by all means sit this one out. Don't wade into waters you're not

> **Don't be insincere and opportunistic. Start with a grounding in what you believe in and care about.**

prepared to stand in for a while. But if there is a fire in your belly, then get going. Where possible, start with actions and follow with words. This is what we've been talking about thus far in the previous chapters. Done with sincerity, commitment, and sensitivity to the right considerations, there is no reason to expect a cynical reaction.

LEADING UNDER FIRE TAKEAWAYS

We've walked around three fair and important challenges to engaging in social issues, and there's a good chance you'll hear them from your boss or your board. Even if you don't, the concerns are valid, and by challenging yourself with those questions, you will sharpen your thinking and strengthen your commitment, or you'll realize that you're getting a little far out over your skis and recalibrate your level of engagement.

Here are some questions to consider as you're playing devil's advocate and addressing possible objections to engaging in broader issues:

- How would you answer the basic question, "How does this issue connect with us and our brand?"

- What are the opportunity costs of supporting a values/issues/purpose initiative?

- What are the quantifiable and unquantifiable considerations that create both risk and opportunity for the brand and the organization?

- Fast-forward five years and imagine the possible futures in which you have consistently weighed in on this issue versus stayed on the sidelines: How do they compare?

- What is the overlap between interest in the issue and your key customer segment? Your emerging customer segments?

- Are you vulnerable to looking like a bandwagon-hopper? Do you have a consistent record of behavior that supports your view? Are you prepared to begin one?

CHAPTER 9

GET READY FOR WHEN IT HITS THE FAN

January 27, 2017—President Trump signs an executive order banning entry into the United States by nationals of seven Muslim-majority countries, causing chaos in major airports.

January 28, 2017—Thousands flood New York's JFK Airport to protest the ban, causing traffic jams and forcing the governor to reopen the discontinued train service to the airport.

4:55 p.m.—The New York Taxi Workers Alliance, an AFL-CIO affiliate that represents the city's cab drivers, many of whom are immigrants, posts this message on Twitter:

NYTWA drivers call for one hour work stoppage @ JFK airport today 6 PM to 7 PM to protest #muslimban! #nobannowall

7:36 p.m.—Uber issues the following tweet:

Surge pricing has been turned off at #JFK Airport. This may result in longer wait times. Please be patient.

7:49 p.m.—Logan Green, CEO of Uber's competitor Lyft, tweets:

Lyft has worked hard to create an inclusive, diverse and conscientious community where all our drivers and passengers feel welcome.

Trump's immigration ban is antithetical to both Lyft's and our nation's core values.

9:04 p.m.—One of thousands of outraged consumer tweets:

way to scab @Uber_NYC thanks for reminding me to delete the app.

i had mostly switched to lyft already but now i'm done for good. it takes longer to get a car but i can wait

11:17 p.m.—A #DeleteUber movement gathers momentum in social media. Another irate consumer tweets:

The heroic cab drivers of @NYTWA stood with refugees against Trump today while @Uber_NYC made $ off it. #DeleteUber

January 29, 2017—Uber responds:

> *Last tweet not meant to break strike. Our CEO's statement opposing travel ban and compensating those impacted: http://t.uber.com/eo*

When the dust settled weeks later, over 200,000 customers had deleted the Uber app from their phones, and Kalanick had resigned from Trump's CEO Council, one of a series of events ultimately culminating in his ouster from the company.

This series of missteps by Uber illustrates the nature of brand crises in the #FakeNews Era: the speed of development, the inflammatory social media environment, and the importance of values transparency. The truth is that Uber suspended surge pricing in that moment because they wanted to avoid the appearance of profiting at the expense of the striking yellow-cab drivers. Their hearts actually were in the right place. But in this case, as in most, good intentions were not enough.

To begin with, look at the difference between the tweets from Uber and from Lyft, mere minutes apart. Uber used a corporate handle to communicate the news of the pricing change, with no explanation of why, no connection to any motivating principle or value, and certainly no reference to the huge event going on at that very moment. It was left to the reader to intuit why Uber made this move.

Lyft's message, by contrast, came from its CEO directly and made a bold, clear statement of Lyft's values and support for the protesters. There's no mistaking where the company stands on the immigration question and the related demonstration—especially when the words come straight from the top guy's lips (or fingertips).

Next, when the stuff does start to hit the fan, look at the damage control effort by Uber: a fairly clinical and terse message with a link to a separate post on Facebook. This linked message was a copy of a wordy e-mail Kalanick had previously sent to employees about the travel ban, talking about how Uber helped its employees affected by the ban, why Kalanick thought it was a good idea to be on Trump's council, and more. Even after the example of the more heartfelt and empathetic note from Lyft, Uber's explanatory tweet is unmoving, with no references to values or beliefs. And rather than addressing the issue in the venue where it first blew up, the post asks readers to shift to Facebook and wade through a memo that contained no mention of the strike and the freeze on surge pricing but did contain lots of discussion of peripheral other stuff.

The last major point is that Uber appears to have failed to consider the overall context in which this event occurred: a consistent history of aggressive and arguably tone-deaf business practices; a total absence of any communications or other evidence of company values or purpose beyond profit; a deficit of goodwill among pretty much anyone who might end up as a character witness in the court of public opinion; and a savvy competitor poised to take advantage of every misstep and play the role of hero to Uber's villain. If Uber had more fully appreciated the critical mass of all these contextual considerations, they might have been moved to take a much more thoughtful and direct approach to containing the growing crisis.

With this cautionary tale, let's look now at how you

> **Let's look now at how you prepare for, assess, and respond to any turbulence that threatens to swamp your brand in these stormy times.**

prepare for, assess, and respond to any turbulence that threatens to swamp your brand in these stormy times. The arenas of reputation management and crisis planning and response are certainly well-developed, and there are any number of great resources to provide granular guidance and templates. My focus here is not to reinvent the reputation management wheel but rather to look at those key processes with an eye toward the new critical considerations for the new realities of the #FakeNews Era.

LEADERSHIP MOVES BEFORE THE STORM HITS YOU

Leadership Moves Before the Storm Hits You:

- Anticipate the danger zones
- Develop a playbook
- Create the communications plan
- Build the content
- Enroll your key influencers
- Check yourself
- Practice, practice, practice
- Tune your radar
- Set your metrics
- Track your brand
- Socialize the learning

Anticipate the danger zones

Gather a cross-functional group—operations, marketing, PR, HR, legal, regulatory, or whatever other functions are relevant. Include select outsiders who can represent the points of view of potential critics, supporters, and other stakeholders in your activities. Go through structured exercises to identify potential flashpoints, how the scenarios might play out, and who might weigh in with what agenda. What interest groups might suddenly call you to account? What operational incidents could take on social or political significance? What are the employee-related risks—either in terms of issues important to them or actions they may take in your name? As you do this war-gaming, assess these scenarios for likelihood and potential damage to the brand and the business.

Develop a playbook

Most companies have some sort of crisis communications plan, but if yours is like most of the places I've worked, it has lots of blank lines in it, it's probably way too long and complicated, and it's likely sitting on a pretty dusty shelf. Now is the time to make it a real, live playbook that can actually drive action when the time comes. This plan needs to spell out roles and responsibilities, such as who fields press calls, how to communicate internally, how decisions get made, and more. We'll go into more detail on some of these points later. Perhaps most importantly, the playbook has to be brief, simple, and accessible. It should be living, continuously updated, and easily available through digital channels everywhere. When Twitter is blowing up and the CEO is freaking out, you don't want people leafing through a fifty-page binder trying to find the section that tells them not to say "No comment" to *The Wall Street Journal.*

> When Twitter is blowing up and the CEO is freaking out, you don't want people leafing through a fifty-page binder trying to find the section that tells them not to say "No comment" to *The Wall Street Journal.*

Create the communications plan

A core part of the playbook will be a guide for communications, both internal and external.

You need to specify how creation of communications will happen: who crafts the message, who reviews and approves it, and where in the organization it comes from. As we saw in the Uber example earlier, there can be a massive difference in the responses to a simple message, driven not only by the wordsmithing but also by something as seemingly subtle as what mailbox it comes from.

It's important also to specify how communications will flow internally. When crisis hits, you'll need to make sure it's clear how to get the right people on board, both for decision governance and for getting the appropriate subject matter experts on the case. Not least of all, you want to ensure that no critical stakeholder is surprised by first hearing about the crisis on CNN.

Build the content

You can't wait until you're under the gun to get your story together. Plan ahead and get the facts, figures, storylines, and other critical support information that you'll need well in advance of a crisis. These points need to be simple, clear, and credible. Wherever possible, leverage facts, data, and other pieces of evidence that can't be debated. When that's not possible, make sure to keep the points tightly focused on the core message and without extraneous detail. Leverage input from your cross-functional team and, even more importantly, from friendly members of external groups. You'll want to test out your proof points and language with them ahead of time, using them as proxies for a less friendly audience. You can even conduct formal research ahead of time to nail the nuances of language. The subtlest shading of word choice can have a major effect on how messages are received, both internally and externally.

A key caution here: remember that you are not your audience. You and your colleagues will likely not be the best litmus test for how to manage a critical, high-emotion flashpoint among an audience very different from you. Your team may be very oriented around logic and data, or comfortable with complexity and nuance. At the very least, as we discussed in previous chapters, you can't hope to understand all the potential sensitivities worth considering. So don't assume that the explanation that moves you will prove as compelling to the public. That's why it's critical to pre-check your story with the right proxies.

Enroll your key influencers

When things go bad, you don't want to be all alone facing the villagers carrying the torches and pitchforks; you want to have allies in the crowd who will speak up for you and tell your story in their voice. But this won't happen unless you take the time to enroll them in advance. That means carefully thinking through, issue by issue, who stands to play a meaningful role in turning the tide of public opinion: thought leaders, associations, interest groups, social media influencers, and of course relevant members of the news media. Create a map of who they are, where they play, and what issues connect you to them. Develop and execute a plan for educating them, engaging them, providing them with your talking points, and sowing the seeds of a positive disposition toward your brand. Otherwise, when called upon to weigh in, they will be filling the empty vessel called "Your Values and Intentions" with their own thoughts in the heat of the moment, and you probably won't get the benefit of the doubt.

Check yourself

It's far too easy to wrap yourself in a cause for good, only to discover later that you're not exactly a poster child for virtue yourself—whether because of some incidents in your organization's past, the actions of an overseas subsidiary, or a set of products that come with squirrelly fine print. As you're moving forward with your agenda, make sure to take a tough and honest look at yourself and your history to identify any warts or vulnerabilities that may surface. Correct them if they still exist and be prepared to convincingly take responsibility for them if they're already in your rearview mirror.

Also, be proactive in setting up internal radar and alarms to make sure you stay on track with whatever values or mission you've aligned to. You have a lot of buzzwords working against you here—agile, decentralized, real-time, empowered—all good stuff of course, but these approaches also raise the odds of a misstep happening outside the chain of decision-making governance. Put in place a culture and language that enables all employees to raise their hands or punch a button if they see something going offtrack. You want the bells going off internally well before any alarm is raised in the public sphere, and your employees are your best and first line of defense in dousing fires before they get out of control.

Practice, practice, practice

Chances are you've been through some sort of media training. I personally believe you can't spend too much time training and practicing for public speaking generally and media communication specifically. As in combat, biology makes everything more challenging, when the adrenaline is pumping and emotions are running high in a tense encounter. The more communication skills you can drive into muscle memory, the more likely it is you'll get through a crisis without fumbling a message or ratcheting up the controversy. While media training typically focuses on skills like message clarity, organization, and bridging from question to talking point, in the

#FakeNews Era there's even more to it. You'll now need to channel your inner Tom Hanks to convey the authentic, human empathy that consumers crave. This comes down to word choice, vocal delivery, body language—all the tools that either say, "I'm a real human being delivering a sincere message from the heart," or, "I'm a corporate tool trying to sell you a line."

Tune your radar

More and more companies are establishing social listening centers—a command center where a team tracks the various social media for messages relevant to the organization. The benefits of such an operation are many: spotting opportunities for positive brand engagement; handling customer service breakdowns in near-real time; gathering competitive intelligence; picking up clues for innovation; and much more. Social listening is particularly important for managing reputations in this challenging environment. Given the speed with which negative momentum builds, you must have your radar tuned constantly to the right frequencies to keep you ahead of trouble. There are many ways to do this, from fully staffed, internal command centers that look like NASA mission control to more automated and outsourced solutions. But one way or another, you need to keep an ear to the ground.

Set your metrics

Naturally there's too much going on in social media to listen and respond to everything, so you'll need to be thoughtful about how you structure metrics to guide your actions. First, you'll need to decide what to listen for—what keywords to pick up and report on. Include mentions of your brand, company, products, and key executives. Load in the issues, themes, and topics that could represent the start of a social media crisis. Be sure also to include key competitors in your tracking. Aside from the intelligence value, we've seen that controversies surrounding one brand can impair the brand health of others in its category. During United's passenger-dragging episode, airline brands generally took a hit in consumer favorability. When Wells Fargo was found to have created thousands of phony accounts, other bank brands sank as well. After selecting your keywords, specify your thresholds for escalation and response. You'll want to have clear guidelines for who gets notified and what actions are triggered at what pace of negative mentions per hour. This is not a decision that should be made ad hoc by whoever happens to be sitting at the social media listening center when trouble starts brewing.

Track your brand

Having just encouraged you to set up a social listening infrastructure, I'll now tell you to listen judiciously. It's very easy to get too spun up over a set of tweets and lose perspective on what represents passing noise versus an enduring problem. There's something about seeing posts from real humans that is somehow more alarming than clinical stats from a consumer call center. I've often seen executives grow both overexcited and overanxious at what amounts to relatively small numbers of posts in social media, compared to the large number of phone calls a major marketer typically gets. Also, just as you aren't your customer, the guy ranting on Twitter isn't necessarily your customer, either. The epicenter of the moral outrage you're hearing may be well outside your key market segment, in which case the brand and business risk may be less than they appear. The key is to do your social listening but also to calibrate using what you see in your more strategic brand metrics: awareness, favorability, key equities, etc. All too frequently, though, funding for brand tracking gets deprioritized to where it becomes a semi-annual or even annual event, so this kind of real-time calibration is often not possible. There are cost-efficient options out there to get a more real-time read on the state of your brand—Morning Consult, for example—and I encourage you to implement some tool for assessing early warning signs of impacts on your brand.

Socialize the learning

Create avenues for disseminating the key learning you derive from social listening and brand tracking. This can take the form of reports circulated on a regular basis, or dashboards available through various solutions vendors. Another very valuable tool can be video screens placed strategically around the office to ensure that associates become familiar with the metrics and attuned to the ongoing consumer dialogue. An intriguing digital screen can be a great way to pique the interest of curious managers and enroll them in the marketing agenda. When we built our social listening center at Hershey, we placed it in a high-traffic corridor to ensure maximum exposure and drive interest and engagement from the marketing teams. Particularly important is making sure the executive suite gets exposed to the data. The more they become familiar with the media and the metrics, the better able they'll be to productively engage in problem-solving when crisis hits, without misinterpreting or overreacting to the inputs.

LEADING UNDER FIRE
TAKEAWAYS

The key to deftly and efficiently handling a brand crisis starts with preparing in advance. What you desperately want to avoid is a room full of stressed-out executives trying to formulate policy, conduct damage control, and communicate calmly in the midst of a crisis. Here are some questions to guide you as you prepare for a stormy day:

- What are the likely trouble spots that could emerge around your brand? Think about issues related to interest groups, employees, supply chains, and customer segments. What would your most severe critic call out?

- Do you have a clear, simple crisis plan that can be effectively put into action by a stressed-out employee? Is there a complete documentation of names, roles, and processes?

- Have you laid out the protocol for how to communicate when crisis hits, both internally and externally?

- What are the key data points, facts, and proof points you need to have at your fingertips to effectively address the scenarios you developed?

- What vulnerabilities do you have in your past or current operation that could undermine your credibility in the issues you're embracing?

- Do you have infrastructure and processes in place to monitor the environment in real time and deliver the right intelligence for rapid response to an emerging crisis?

CHAPTER 10

HOW TO RESPOND UNDER FIRE

Your cell phone goes off at midnight, just as you were capping off an evening of binge-watching that new series on Netflix. Your social media manager is on the line telling you that Twitter is blowing up, the negative mentions have reached the preset DEFCON 2 level, and the team is starting to sweat. The summary she sends you tells the story of a well-intentioned ad campaign setting off a firestorm of controversy that nobody predicted. And then, sure enough, an e-mail from the CEO pops up asking you what the hell is going on.

As with developing a crisis management plan, there are a world of experts, books, and templates available on the subject of managing a reputation crisis. I won't compete with them but will touch on the major areas with a focus on what you need to particularly get right when things go wrong for brands in the #FakeNews Era.

No Matter What You Decide:

- Be Thoughtful
- Be Quick
- Take Ownership
- Be Real
- Be Measured
- Follow Through

1. BE THOUGHTFUL

In the early stages of a brewing crisis, there may be high levels of anxiety and strong urges to leap into action—to thunderously deny, weepily apologize, launch counterattacks, or otherwise release the PR hounds. This is the point where a cool head needs to prevail, and you need to do a thoughtful—though quick—evaluation of the situation in order to determine the appropriate response.

The most important question is whether this is a minor squall that will pass or a major storm that poses a meaningful threat of damage to the brand and business. As you look at all the signals coming from your social feeds, start by grounding them in benchmarks and leverage the available analytics to put the data into context.

Triangulate the social signal with your brand tracking systems: Does the negative sentiment expressed online seem to be having an effect on any critical brand metrics? Very often, Twitter outrage does not end up moving brand favorability, so you'll want to be careful not to overreact if the noise does not seem to be generating any damage.

Go deeper on the source of the negative sentiment to see whether it's in a core or fringe market segment in order to assess how serious the fallout might be. The irate posters may fall well outside of your target and may represent little to no revenue risk—or they may be your core customer segment that represents the heart of the business. Wells Fargo, for example, saw brand erosion in its lucrative retiree segment following the revelations of fraudulent account openings, according to Morning Consult data, spelling more serious risks to its brand and business health.

Consider these points when responding under fire:

- The nature of the issue
- The impact of the issue
- The broader context
- The values affected

Most critical at this point is to analyze the strength and virality of crisis: Is it a brief flurry of indignation, or an enduring problem that poses meaningful brand and business risk? The number and pace of consumer posts is one indication. To thoroughly assess the gravity of the situation and calibrate the appropriate response, consider these points:

- **The nature of the issue**—Is this a one-time event, like a single customer service fail, or is it a more evergreen issue that will provide ongoing fodder for controversy, such as an objectionable policy hardwired into the business? Is this a sin of commission, such as an offending ad campaign, or one of omission, such as failure to speak up and declare yourself on a hot issue? Is it a question of misinterpretation, where your otherwise positive intent and actions were seen in the wrong light? Patience and restraint may be the answer for a controversy over a one-time sin of omission, whereas an egregious misstep or an enduring issue may need more active intervention.

- **The emotional impact of the issue**—Some events simply have more visceral and viral power. Are you facing conceptual criticisms delivered in text, or are there photos, videos, or company artifacts flying around the Internet? A video of a bloodied and unconscious airline passenger or an abusive CEO rant pack a lot of punch and will likely have more staying power and emotional impact than a less visual irate post.

- **The broader context**—Have you been in this fix before? Is it part of an ongoing drumbeat of negativity around your brand? An event that is part of a continuing saga is likely to pose a greater risk as a critical mass of negativity builds. Wells Fargo is the poster child for a story that simply does not end, with an ongoing series of damaging revelations. Does it play into an ongoing storyline about your industry? Competitive brands are often tarred with the same brush, and general industry critiques as well as individual company controversies can bleed over into the brand health of an otherwise unblemished competitor. As we saw with Uber, the broader context in which the event occurs should dictate how actively you respond.

- **The values affected**—What is the core value or belief that lies at the heart of the accusation? There is a spectrum of consumer response, from vague disapproval through raging moral condemnation, and the decibel level depends to a great degree on the value that was triggered. Some issues are so profound and universal that they demand a clear, vocal, and rapid response, regardless of other considerations, and there can be no "waiting it out" without suffering consequences.

On the basis of these considerations, you'll need to decide whether you're going to stay silent and monitor closely or go into action to manage and contain the crisis.

2. BE QUICK

Having just counseled you to avoid knee-jerk reactions, I will now also urge you to act quickly if indeed you have chosen to act. Internet time is measured in hours, if that. Time to response is now a closely watched metric, whether for companies, celebrities, or politicians commenting on theirs or others' transgressions. Witness the criticism of Trump as the public waited for him to condemn the Charlottesville marches, or of male movie stars who were slower to speak out about Harvey Weinstein's history of sexual assault. One of the major criticisms of how United handled their PR crisis was the time it took for any meaningful communication to emerge from company leadership. As I talked with CMOs whose brands were caught up in controversy, many described executing what they thought was a rapid response, only to discover they were too late. A mere couple of days later, they'd already been declared guilty, with no more opportunities for pleading their case.

Very often, companies don't have the benefit of all the facts and inputs needed for their complete and final story. This can lead them to adopt a painful silence or, even worse, the dreaded "no comment." It's important to communicate even if you aren't able to present your most buttoned-up and complete case—you must show that you're aware, listening hard, digging in fast, and sincerely care about the issue. This doesn't constitute admitting guilt or undermining a more informed subsequent response—it simply buys you the time and permission to get your ducks in a row without incurring further damage.

Ensure also that you respond in the venue in which the firestorm began. If outrage breaks out on Twitter and you respond in a press release or a webpage, the tree is falling in the wrong forest, and no one will hear it. Uber's response to the JFK Airport #DeleteUber campaign asked the energized Twitter community to bounce over to Facebook rather than containing the fire where it first broke out. A complete response may well include communications in a number of venues, but be sure to at least do a good job of telling your story in the place the trouble began.

3. TAKE OWNERSHIP

If you face a situation where you did indeed commit some form of sin, then take complete and unambiguous ownership of it. Every word uttered and printed will be parsed, examined, and mined for insincerity and misdirection. Your goal here is to make the problem go away as quickly as possible, not to explore the many nuances, shades, and subtleties of accountability. The best and only way to make it go away quickly is to leave no doubt that you're shouldering responsibility and that you're not trying to cloud the issue or shift the blame. *Do not* execute the non-apology apology, which we've seen so often around the #MeToo sexual harassment episodes: "I'm kinda sorry, but not really cuz I didn't totally do it ... at least not quite like she said ... to her, anyway." *Saturday Night Live* beautifully captured the companion dodge, the I-support-you-non-apology: "Lots of women are brave but this one is ... um ... a liar." Apologies need to be simple, complete, and sincere.

Think also about where the buck needs to stop. Don't try to shunt the blame to the junior-most person involved in the misstep. Make it clear that the senior-most executives embrace the problem and see it as a collective failing and approach the solution at that level.

In the course of taking ownership, tie back to your most fundamental values and beliefs, either in terms of where you went wrong or how you plan to be better going forward. Doing this will demonstrate an appreciation for the depth of the issue, as well as a sincerity around your intentions to improve. United Airlines, in an early explanation for the passenger clubbing incident, cited a need to "re-accommodate" fliers. A far more effective approach would have been to lose the deflecting jargon and acknowledge a fundamental breakdown in their commitment to "fly friendly: warm and welcoming."

These same principles also apply if your objective is not to apologize but rather to stand proud and reaffirm your position. Ground your position in the values and beliefs you hold dear, and simply and clearly articulate the most fundamental "why" behind your position and your actions.

4. BE REAL

Most of the crises brands face in the #FakeNews Era are fundamentally about human values and therefore human feelings: disrespected, marginalized, insulted, threatened, fearful, morally indignant, and more. You start out behind the eight ball, because you are a corporate brand, already viewed with some degree of cynicism and suspicion. You'll have to make an explicit, concerted effort to speak, write, and sound like genuine humans with an empathetic response to a human issue. This means no lingo, no tortured legalese, no protective caveats—don't say, "re-accommodate passenger" when you really mean, "make room for our crew." This also means choosing your spokespeople carefully—some have a gift for empathetic communication, and some simply come across as a bit cold and mechanical, especially under stress. This is why it's so critical to conduct the training and practice we discussed earlier. Refer to company values, and use "I" and "we" statements.

Chobani founder Hamdi Ulukaya is one of the most forward-leaning CEOs when it comes to engaging in broader social issues. As he approaches controversial topics to consider the company position, Ulukaya says that he tries to think not as a brand or a company but as a human, as a neighbor or family member considering the welfare of loved ones. "When it comes to issues that we totally care about, we'll react honestly. So it's not a brand reaction, it's a human reaction." If the human basis for your controversial position can come through in a heartfelt communication during a crisis, you will be in a much better position to effectively address the issues and move past them.

5. BE MEASURED

A great temptation when under fire is to shoot back, or at the very least to defend and justify. When your mission is to make a crisis go away quickly, these are generally the last things you want to do. As you craft messages and speak publicly, it's critical to avoid any language or tonality that will further fan the flames of indignation. Remember that the audience is already running in the emotional red zone and looking for reasons to disbelieve you and catch you in the act of missing the point. It's all too easy to add new fuel to the fire with new arguments or counterpoints that will inevitably be criticized—all of which only prolongs the crisis.

Just ask Matt Damon, who generally seems to be a pretty well-intentioned guy. As the #MeToo movement swept through Hollywood, he voiced his support for the growing awareness and focus on the problem. He also added the idea that there was a "spectrum" of behavior, from butt-patting to outright abuse and rape—all of which he called inappropriate, but not all representing the same level of crime or calling for the same level of punishment. While perhaps intellectually defensible, his comments brought a landslide of criticism from friends, colleagues, and the general public. This was simply not a topic, and that was not a time, where he was viewed as having permission to parse out distinctions—and he wasn't even apologizing for anything he did in the first place. Stay conscious of the potential for unintentionally tripping the trigger of a new problem, and remain focused on providing the clearest, simplest, most unambiguous communication that does nothing to escalate or prolong the issue.

6. FOLLOW-THROUGH

As I've emphasized in earlier chapters, consistency of action is key, and never more so than in the aftermath of a crisis. Whether you are confidently reaffirming your position or sincerely apologizing and committing to a better path, you must walk that walk. This will start with a thorough and honest review of how you got there in the first place. Whether fairly or wrongly accused, a series of events led to you being in the hot seat, so you'll want to conduct an open-minded after-action review to understand how it happened.

Review the policies that might have been at the root of a misstep. For example, do gate agents not have enough flexibility to creatively entice passengers to happily give up their seats? Do cost-containment goals conflict with desired standards of customer care?

Or is it a culture issue, whereby the core values of the company have not been widely and deeply instilled in the organization? Are there mixed messages being sent from the very top? Does management extol the value of empathy but place operational efficiency above all other considerations?

Likewise, if the issue was a blameless misunderstanding, you'll still want to understand how that arose. Did you not have sufficient relationships with members of the affected community? Does your staff lack the diversity of perspective necessary to spot potential misfires of language or context? Did your monitoring fail to pick up signs of a miscue early enough to correct and contain it before a broader outbreak?

Whatever you discover in these reviews, you'll want to communicate what you've learned and what you plan to do differently going forward. Then make sure that you follow through in your actions and make them appropriately visible to demonstrate your sincerity and progress in keeping your word.

LEADING UNDER FIRE
TAKEAWAYS

Nothing tests your mettle like managing a full-blown brand crisis. You'll need to carefully understand the issue, calmly implement your response plan, and focus on containing the issue effectively. Here are some questions to guide you through this process:

- What kind of crisis are you looking at? Does it appear to be a brief episode, or does it have the signs of an ongoing story that is likely to gather strength over time?

- What's the nature of the issue: a misstep that calls for an apology, or a difference of opinion that calls for a reaffirmation?

- Where did the issue start, and how quickly can you respond with your initial communications?

- How can you most genuinely display empathy and come across as real people behind the brand?

- What are the hot-button words or concerns that you must avoid tripping over as you communicate?

- What must you examine in terms of policies, practices, or culture that can help you avoid stepping on similar landmines in the future?

- What consistent action must you take in the wake of the crisis to demonstrate your sincerity and avoid recurring episodes?

CHAPTER 11

IS THIS REALITY HERE TO STAY?

As I've talked about the challenges for brands in the #FakeNews Era while speaking and consulting around the country, one question constantly comes up: Will all of these turbulent new realities settle down at some point, perhaps when the political arena shifts, or is this the new normal? Buried in the question I can hear

> There's absolutely a new normal.

an unstated but fervent wish for a return to a time less fraught with risk, where brand owners don't have a baseline anxiety around where and when they will be caught up in a swirl of controversy or called out as a spineless benchwarmer.

Some trends come and go, while other changes represent a structural shift that calls for a fundamental rethinking of strategies and retooling of tactics. So, should we learn to get comfortable with this new reality for the long haul? In late 2017 and early 2018, I posed this question to some of the brightest people I know who spend their days thinking about brands and reputations. They represent a broad spectrum of CMOs, insights experts, agency heads, PR professionals, and academics. Rather than compile and digest their comments, I'll let them each speak in their own words to provide you the full richness of their insights. And although they come at the question from highly varied perspectives, their comments all share a consistent theme running throughout: Get used to it.

> **A consistent theme running throughout: Get used to it.**

HELAINE KLASKY, U.S. VICE PRESIDENT AND CHAIR OF PUBLIC AFFAIRS AND CRISIS MANAGEMENT PRACTICE, BURSON-MARSTELLER

Broadly speaking, society will never simply return to how it used to be before President Trump. He has caused a seismic shift in the tone of Washington, politics, and public communications more generally. There has always been an undercurrent of harsh divisiveness in our society, but Trump took that fire that was at a low burn and turned it up so high that people will now just keep digging in. Many will want to return to an environment of greater civility and compromise in public life, but I think it will take a long time to get there. What was latent is now blatant, and that's not been a good thing for the country.

At our firm, we identified 225 individual campaign promises that Trump made, and we've been tracking his progress against them ever since. He's actually doing what he said he'd do. So you need to ask yourself, if Trump issued an executive order on these ten agenda items, things that he's promised but that you might have discounted, how would it affect you? What would you do? Who would you involve in your response?

We're seeing a lot of legislative and regulatory activity at the city, state, and federal level—all of which has a meaningful effect on brands. Not just the issues of how the public brand responds to the situation, but even getting into the fundamental way you do business. Whether it's changes to environmental regulation with little notice, or changes in supply chain issues or immigration policies, it all impacts the way you run your business and thereby your brand.

Most of all, corporate leaders need to be prepared and ready to react with little notice. We live in a world with 24-hour news cycle where opinions are formed by a tweet. You have to be ready, be nimble, and keep an eye out as you might end up in the cross-fire.

MARYAM BANIKARIM, GLOBAL CMO, HYATT HOTELS CORPORATION

At Hyatt, we were getting ready to celebrate the 50th anniversary of Hyatt Regency Atlanta with a campaign called "Come Together." We were highlighting a story from the brand's past with the help of the Atlantic Media Group. Fifty years ago, in August, Hyatt Regency Atlanta had been the only hotel that opened its doors to Martin Luther King Jr. and his Southern Christian Leadership Conference. As a company that believes that understanding is what the world needs, we wanted to showcase this moment in our company's history. We were scheduled to launch our campaign, and then the Charlottesville protests happened. We had to pause and think about whether we stayed the course or whether we should make a different decision. After a lot of deliberation, we decided to keep to our launch plan. Our date had been pegged to the actual date of the Southern Christian

Conference gathering fifty years ago to the day. And we thought our message of "Coming Together" was even more relevant. We believed we should not shy away from that message. You don't control everything in life, and when things happen that are bigger than you, you need to pause and reconsider what you're doing. What's critical is having a team that brings diversity of thought in those moments, because they can help look at things from different perspectives.

DENISE KARKOS, CMO, TD AMERITRADE

I think about trends a lot, from clothing to hairstyles to management practices and somewhat lazily have been known to say, "It all comes back around." In view of recent trends, I've put more thought into this notion of what is cyclical vs evolutionary in nature, and perhaps it comes down to what's superficial vs foundational.

The foundational shift is an empowered consumer. Social media has given them a voice, and technology strengthens its signal. As our society progresses and diversifies, there are weightier topics to discuss. This does not seem like a cycle or a trend that will eventually settle down.

Brands that used to use their hefty budgets to drive sales now have to wield their power to contribute to society. The work to be done here involves an introspective look at the entire ecosystem so that the brand promise is simply a mirror to the internal operations of the brand. A more empowered and emboldened consumer will reward brands that get this right.

ANTHONY JOHNDROW, COFOUNDER AND CEO, REPUTATION ECONOMY ADVISORS

There's a sense that maybe this will be over soon—but I don't think it will be at all. We'll probably see this same polarizing dynamic a lot in the 2018 midterm elections. You've already seen other politicians using Trump's techniques and tactics to get attention—the rock throwing and the like. You'll see the media start to do the same thing. They've been on their back foot for a while. And not just fringe media—the mainstream media will get more polarized as well. They'll be asking, "What's our technique for getting more visibility?" The crazy and outlandish and extremely polarizing will be the path forward for them as well. That's how you make money; that's how you get attention.

Brand owners have to look for their moment. They need to be ready to take advantage of it. You need to have a clear sense of what you stand for. A lot of organizations are woefully unprepared for that. North Face and REI, for example, knew what they stood for and were ready to jump in when the moment happened. Going forward, consumers will continue to expect brands to engage in the social/political arena, but those expectations will increase for specificity in values and cause—broad-brush purpose won't work. You'll need to stand for something extremely specific and clear.

JEFF ROSENBLUM, CO-PRESIDENT OF QUESTUS, AUTHOR, AND DOCUMENTARY FILMMAKER

Is Trump cause or effect of all these new dynamics? Either way, at the end of the day, Trump is a master of the new art of branding. I'm not a fan of his as a human being or a leader, but you have to give him credit for mastering the new media landscape.

What he realized during the election was that his job was not to *buy* media effectively. His job was to help companies *sell* media effectively. Hillary, on the other hand, tried to do what Obama did well—put the right message at the right place at the right time by leveraging data and social media. There's nothing wrong with that at face value except that interruptive ads are not nearly as effective as immersive content. People are more likely to die in a plane crash than actually read a display ad. But millions of people tuned in to Fox News, CNN, and Twitter to hear what Trump had to say. Trump built his brand through content—unique and powerful content, if we're being honest. You can say it was outlandish or even unethical, but it connected with his audience and accomplished his goals.

So, what does this lesson mean for brands? We live in a new reality. We're asking interruptive advertising to do too much. This isn't about the death of advertising—that false eulogy has been given before. But brands need to create content that people will go out of their way to participate in and share with others. They need to use magnets, not megaphones.

Most importantly, brands need to stand for something very specific. They need to build immersive content that brings their value system to life. They need to create experiences that empower people and enrich their lives.

Patagonia is almost the exact polar opposite of Trump in regard to value systems. But, like Trump, they stand for something clearly, they stay on message, and they create extensive content that empowers the audience. For Patagonia, it's all about defending the environment.

But many brands have misanalyzed Patagonia's efforts, thinking it's a green story. While that works for Patagonia, people don't wake up in the morning wanting brands to hug the trees and save the manatees. It would be nice if every brand did, but it's not realistic.

It's really about this: recognizing that people are selfish. Not in a bad way, but in a very natural and human way. We want what's best for us. We want to maximize the return that we get on our money, time, and effort. So brands need to create content that improves people's lives, one small step at a time. For Patagonia's audience, it's about defending the environment.

That approach isn't always the most effective, however. Take REI. They ran their "Opt Outside" program and closed on Black Friday to encourage us all to go outside and enjoy nature. That's a nice piece of content that helped with REI's positioning in the middle and the top of the funnel. But the brand that I personally purchase from is Back-Country.com. They have a team of "Gearheads" who are available via chat, text, phone calls, and e-mail. Whatever sport you are interested in, at whatever skill level you have, these Gearheads provide incredible extensive advice about which products will meet your needs.

So, if you really love the outdoors, Patagonia and REI are appealing brands because they have similar value systems. Back-Country.com also values the outdoors, but improves the audience's life on a one-to-one basis by helping them make smarter purchases. They connect the middle and the bottom of the funnel, whereas REI's "Opt Outside" program is more about the middle and the top of the funnel.

It's funny to start talking about Donald Trump and finish by talking about outdoor brands. Their perspectives on the world couldn't be more different. I personally love REI, Patagonia, and BackCountry.com. President Trump really worries me. Yet, we can't argue with branding success. There are great lessons to learn from brands that make an emotional connection, regardless of the audience or the platform.

KEVIN LANE KELLER, E. B. OSBORN PROFESSOR OF MARKETING, TUCK SCHOOL OF BUSINESS, DARTMOUTH COLLEGE

There are so many forces at play. Beyond the social/political angle, the interesting ones in my mind are all the transparencies and knowledge that now characterize the marketplace, and also the tremendous uncertainty that still exists with respect to consumers, competition, and the government. This makes for a fascinating juxtaposition, with privacy also adding to the mix!

I think those forces are going to continue to gain in importance, and the savvy marketers will figure out how to balance these considerations most effectively to build and manage their brands. I also think the transparency and scrutiny faced by brands and companies will sustain and likely increase. It's the nature of the news and media environment. As part of that, and for other reasons, consumers expect more from brands and companies, and younger millennials especially will want to know about the greater good involved—not necessarily a bad trend at all.

In terms of consumer activism and boycotts, I am not quite as sure. Everything I said up until now would suggest that they will increase in importance, but at the same time I am not sure. I think firms will be able to increasingly figure out who is a squeaky wheel and more of a crank and not have to so reflexively respond to every criticism, no matter how unfounded or off the mark it might be.

Lastly, in terms of political expression by brands going forward, I see that being too dangerous for most all brands except those who make political values and statements the core positioning to their brand. I think brand marketers will increase involvement in the other trend of engaging in socially beneficial behavior and their various

PETER HORST

causes and other activities as a much safer platform to be relevant but non-controversial.

RALPH SANTANA, EVP AND CMO, HARMAN INTERNATIONAL

With an explosion of new and hyper-interactive media platforms and democratization of news and commentary, companies and brands are enticed—and arguably expected—to directly engage with their stakeholders on topics and issues that may touch ethical, social, moral, and emotional topics. More than anything, we as marketers, communicators, and employers must maintain our values and authenticity, staying true to who we are and what we stand for versus trying to be something we're not or—worse—artificial and opportunistic. We do this not by reacting to or capitalizing on the day's headlines but by consistently and steadily reinforcing our values and identity.

No company or brand is immune to controversy or conflict in an increasingly diverse and vocal world, but authentic branding and ongoing transparent communications with employees, shareholders, and customers will build trust and provide valuable insulation when issues arise. Maintaining credibility and trust is pivotal for businesses in today's ultra-social digital age, and, like any healthy, productive relationship, we are well-served to invest the time and resources to be honest and open and stay close to our customers—whether they are buying our stock, purchasing our products, or joining our company.

MICHAEL MASLANSKY, CEO,
MASLANSKY + PARTNERS

We're definitely in a new world. Companies face new complexities, like the macro trend that more millennials and others are focused on the values a company communicates, what it stands for, and how it operates. For a while, companies may shrug this off as an edge phenomenon—very important to a small part of the population but not hugely important to the majority. But the real question is which is more important: What the majority thinks, or what a very vocal minority thinks? Here, that minority can and should start to drive corporate behavior.

Another dynamic is the faster-moving reality around polarization and politicization of society, with an administration that is adept at creating controversies that put brands in a position where they have to act or respond.

Is this an enduring change or a temporary phenomenon? The kinds of tactics Trump has used will normalize. You won't have someone who garners so much attention and who consistently creates controversies that require a response. There will likely be fewer instances of someone like Trump putting brands in a position of having to be for or against him. But the issues will be there: the polarized media, the fake news, and the "boycott everything" movements mean that there will be plenty of situations where companies are forced to make a choice between staying silent and making a statement.

In this future, it will be harder to be a big company that's all things to all people—even putting aside the crazy current issues. We've seen it with the bifurcation of many markets between luxury and low cost, where the middle category is the worst place to be. It's easier to be low-cost Southwest Airlines than mass-market American. It's hard to be big and universal. The same will happen with social issues. Companies will be forced to define who they are, and which segments of customers and employees they appeal to. They will not be able to have it all.

NICK PRIMOLA, SVP, HEAD OF INDUSTRY LEADERSHIP AND CMO OF INITIATIVES, ASSOCIATION OF NATIONAL ADVERTISERS (ANA)

Technology has added a hyperspace button to most everything. Whether one's intent is to instigate, motivate, build up, or tear down, it can all be amplified a thousand times through technology, instantly. In real life people are generally civil, and even borderline boring. But insert technology and BOOM—different ballgame. Today's tech enables *anyone*—not just advertisers or the media, but literally anyone—to exploit anyone else's emotional triggers and supplies them with an unlimited tank of gas to press the pedal on to provoke emotions and shape perceptions towards any issue, brand, or idea.

Chief marketing officers find themselves uniquely positioned in the middle. On one hand there's unprecedented opportunity to connect with consumers in a deeply relevant and personal way. On the other hand is the amplified risk of being wrong, which carries potentially boundless consequences to the brand.

Aside from a few brave examples, I've observed that most chief marketing officers are erring on the side of caution. And who can blame them? What used to be executing a simple ad campaign might now feel like walking through a corridor of online ninjas ready to strike anytime from anywhere.

To some extent this has had a positive impact by bringing a new level of integrity to the work itself. Brands have to not just *mean* what they say but also *be* what they say. A brand can't just stand for an idea without also being genuine to that same idea themselves. And it's not just now, by the way … but always and forever ago. It's too easy for anyone with an Internet connection to find out something that happened over twenty or thirty years ago and hold a brand accountable for it today. Just the same, it's too easy for competitors or anyone with a conflicting agenda to find something that suits their narrative to use against any brand. It doesn't matter if it happened now, halfway across the planet or if it happened in ancient history— you're accountable now.

With hyper-transparency so possible, a brand, along with everyone and everything ever associated with it, must be true to its purpose. And aside from the CEO, the chief marketing officer is best positioned to ensure the brand's truth is grounded in the company's core purpose and that the relationship between it and its consumers are aligned in that purpose in a transparent and truthful way.

MARC DE SWAAN ARONS, CMO, KANTAR VERMEER

There's absolutely a new normal. The new normal is transparency. You absolutely are expected to be completely transparent about who you are, what you've done, what you're doing, who you're working with, how you treat people. All the questions that people may ask, you need to proactively volunteer the answers. And if something you are accused of is the truth, then you've got to be willing to face up to it and transform whatever you need to transform to be acceptable. It's a new reality that you need that kind of transparency. There's no negotiating that, it's not a choice. This is, "Wake up, it's the new world you're operating in."

But I don't think that brands created to make, say, clothes cleaner, should feel the need to jump up and start empowering women or cleaning the world. I think Toyota with its Super Bowl ads about disabilities was far over the line—there's nothing about Toyota that is around helping people with disabilities. It's a great cause but it has nothing to do with Toyota. Likewise with the Hyundai Superbowl ad about supporting cancer research. Brands are really out of their depth when they start doing things like that.

The question is, what are you building your brand around? Most brands do build around a human truth—and human truths are almost by definition not political. Everyone wants to be a great mother and a great father. Everybody wants to be a role model. Everybody wants to live comfortably. These are the human truths that the biggest brands have built themselves around, and these are not highly politicized items. When P&G talked about motherhood at the Olympics, that was spot on. That's true, and you can't end up in a political storm when you do that, because it's universal.

JACKSON JEYANAYAGAM, CMO, BOXED

I believe in the very near future, and arguably in this current climate, it's going to be essential for brands to make a choice and stand for *something. Anything.* Just as long as it's authentic to them, with genuine and transparent intent, and they are consistent in terms of how they devote their brand purpose and employee goals against it. Of course, with any cause-related initiative there is always a risk of alienating customers/audiences/investors, but I'm not sure if that's going to really matter in the near future. I believe brands will have their hands forced to take a stand and proactively articulate what it is they believe in.

Now, obviously no consumer is going to pay 50 percent more for a product or service just because they can relate to you. But assuming all things are equal and pricing is somewhat competitive, I can see a very real scenario where your brand ethos trumps a small savings to the customer; perhaps not for commoditized products but most certainly for high-profile brands where shopping at a specific store/ecommerce site or buying a specific product is a reflection of who you are as a consumer (and what you believe in). *That* world, and the inevitable decision for brands to make, is coming very soon … and once generation Z is in the "commerce driver seat," it will be a nonnegotiable.

At Boxed, we knew this was very much a likelihood when we took a stand against the "tampon tax"—a luxury tax placed on feminine hygiene products similar to liquor, in more than 30 states—an important issue raised by an employee. Immediately upon learning about this discrepancy the entire leadership team, including the founders, supported her and the cause by taking action and refunding that tax to any customers shopping with us, who resided in those particular states. It wasn't received well by everybody, however. We saw our fair share of negative comments from consumers saying that the gender gap wasn't an issue and we were creating a solution to a problem that didn't exist; but that's the exact moment where an organization has to make a choice, and we made ours. We were, and continue to be, all in on doing the right thing because we can. Period.

KIM WHITLER, ASSISTANT PROFESSOR, DARDEN SCHOOL OF BUSINESS, UNIVERSITY OF VIRGINIA

Marketers should be the stewards and protectors of the brand. When done correctly, they have a big and aspirational vision of what the brand can be—what it should stand for in the hearts and minds of consumers. To achieve this requires consistent and authentic effort against a specific message delivered over time. The best marketers understand that social- and cause-related marketing should emanate from the brand's behavior over time. Essentially you have to "walk the walk before talking." The worst marketers, unfortunately, look to co-opt a "hot topic" and benefit from it. They talk about an issue when it isn't part of the fabric, value system, or behavior of the brand.

As an example, Audi ran an ad about gender pay inequality last year. It was a powerful message—as any message about women being paid less than men for the same work might be. After watching the ad, I had some fundamental questions. Why does Audi have the right to run this ad? Have they for years and decades been proponents of gender pay equality? Or are they just trying to co-opt a hot topic to sell cars by tapping into an emotional issue? So I went and looked at their board and their senior management team. Almost no women. I looked to see if there was press/news about how they have taken steps at Audi to drive pay equality. Has the CEO ever talked about this topic or seemed to care about it? No. It appeared to me that an advertising agency, approved by Audi's management team, decided to leverage a very emotional and important topic to connect it to Audi and drive positive affect and sales.

MIKE PAUL, PRESIDENT, REPUTATION DOCTOR LLC

Truly thinking and feeling from another person's perspective is the most important tool in the toolbox. Why? Because when you can connect with other human beings that deeply, you build trust and insights others will miss. Trust is the most important currency in marketing and branding worldwide. And you will never build deep trust without active listening, sincere empathy, and the ability to connect deeply with others by knowing their thoughts and feelings as if they are your own.

The average CMO and CEO have many tools on the tool belt to deal with the current environment. But the best tool that they should have ready and sharpened is usually left in the toolbox and is starting to get rusty—that is EQ (emotional intelligence). A moral and an ethical compass. CMOs and CEOs should ask themselves, "If this stakeholder were me or someone important to me, how would I think about this issue from such a deep perspective that I can mirror their thoughts and feelings?" Learn EQ like it's breathing. Practice the ability to think from another person's perspective so they can't be anything but moved when you understand who they are as a person. It's not metrics. Metrics won't solve all the problems. Numbers aren't enough. Know your consumers, know your products, get out there, and know who's using them. Deeply understand why they chose your product.

We heard from a bunch of smart people about where they think this world is going. I'll close now with my parting thoughts on that subject, along with some words of encouragement.

Whether it's politics, consumer trends, or marketing tactics, we seem to move in giant swings of a pendulum. The center of gravity in Congress lurches from left to right and back again in a never-ending cycle of apparent over-corrections and buyer's remorse. Coconut oil goes from nutritional demon to health food to plain old saturated fat. Programmatic media goes from the second coming of marketing efficiency to a brand safety nightmare.

I believe—or more accurately, fervently hope—that we'll see some degree of swing back on some aspects of our present reality. I have to believe that we can't as a nation continue for long at the same fever pitch of rancor and outrage. Perhaps we'll need to exhaust ourselves before we can pause to take a breath and

> Perhaps we'll need to exhaust ourselves before we can pause to take a breath and find a new way to interact with each other and remind ourselves that there is still a tribe called "Americans," and even more importantly "Humans," that deserve our passionate commitment.

find a new way to interact with each other and remind ourselves that there is still a tribe called "Americans," and even more importantly "Humans," that deserve our passionate commitment.

At the same time, I also believe, as the smart people in Chapter 11 generally do, that much of what we're seeing now is in fact the new normal. There are too many powerful currents that have already carved their way through our national psyche to think that we can go back to a reality that seemed safer, where we felt less exposed, challenged, and judged by the world in such fundamental ways.

So get used to it.

Learn how to navigate the new realities and, better yet, take control of them and of your destiny, so you can elevate your brand, your company, and your broader community.

> Learn how to navigate the new realities and, better yet, take control of them and of your destiny, so you can elevate your brand, your company, and your broader community.

The world is too complex and varied for me to give you a simple answer for how to engage in the broader issues that challenge society. What I have tried to do is provide a framework, a language, and guidance for how to think through and execute on a deliberate approach to managing the challenging dynamics facing brand owners. Leaders must decide for themselves, based on the realities of their business model, owners, customers, and tribes, where they can reasonably play on the Brand Risk-Relevance Curve of **values**, **purpose**, **issues**, and **positions**. The only prescription I will give to everyone is to be *intentional* about choosing one of them. The only wrong answer is to do none of them, because doing nothing means you believe we will go back to a kinder, gentler time when all you had to do was make good ads about a good product and the world would leave you alone.

That time is gone, and it isn't coming back.

So start by digging deep and introspectively finding that motivating spark, the fundamental *why* your company deserves to exist. Define and memorialize those values that are so important to you that you'd shed blood for them.

Rally other leaders, your owners, your employees, and other stakeholders to join your tribe of values and purpose and infuse them with the energy of that commitment. Make it clear how those values define the way you will operate and where you would feel compelled to speak up loudly.

It may well be that your business faces a number of realities that limit your freedom in this arena. Pragmatically speaking, maybe you can do no more than ground yourself in **values** and cannot publicly espouse any points of view beyond the confines of your product offering. If that's as far as you can prudently go, then you've done good work and are prepared to manage and survive in the #FakeNews Era—and whatever comes after it. Your values and the culture they create will act as a moral compass and will enable you to respond swiftly and effectively if circumstances call for you to put those values on display.

But I challenge you to ask yourself whether you can do more and go further than quietly ground in your values. Are you letting your fear of the unknown risks cloud your view of the possible benefits of engaging more deeply in the world around your brand? Reject the false premise that says you have to choose between remaining silent or taking a harshly polarizing and political stance. As we've seen in the instances of Unilever, Frito-Lay, Heineken, and others, there is a spectrum of choices in how a brand can engage. There are many ways to leverage the power of your brand voice, your resources, and your creativity to contribute to the world without wading into the minefield of specific policies and polarizing politics. You can make a contribution without making enemies.

And remember, the world expects you to do more.

More importantly, the world needs you to do more.

And I know you're up to it.

Good luck.

We'll all be watching …

Named as one of *Forbes*'s Top 50 Most Influential CMOs, Peter Horst is a Fortune 500 CMO with thirty years of experience across consumer and business products, services, and technology for market leaders such as Capital One, Hershey, General Mills, US WEST (CenturyLink), and TD Ameritrade. He was behind the creation of some of the most iconic brands, products, and award-winning marketing campaigns. Peter now leads CMO Inc., a marketing advisory. He works with companies in a wide range of industries, from technology to financial services to consumer products. Peter helps organizations define their marketing priorities, build powerful brand strategies, sharpen their messaging, and focus their innovation efforts. He has increasingly been called on to assist organizations in defining, aligning, and executing around a broader brand purpose. Peter is a highly rated keynote speaker, contributes to *Forbes* and other publications, and sits on advisory boards for several early stage companies.

As Global CMO of the Hershey Company, Peter was responsible for Hershey's iconic global brands, innovation, creative, media, design, digital advancement, and flagship retail stores.

Previously, Peter served in increasingly responsible executive roles at Capital One, including CMO of Capital One Bank. He was behind the creation and launch of numerous successful products and iconic marketing campaigns, and he led the brand's evolution to be a top-ten bank.

Before Capital One, Peter served as CMO at TruSecure Corporation, a cybersecurity start-up, and as the first CMO at Ameritrade (now TD Ameritrade), where he built that brand and drove fivefold customer growth. Prior to Ameritrade, Peter held marketing leadership positions at US WEST, now CenturyLink, and at General Mills.

Peter earned a BA from Harvard and an MBA from Dartmouth's Tuck School of Business.

For more **BIG THINKING** and **BOLD MOVES**, check out Peter and CMO Inc. at www.**CMOINC**.com